Sound intuition. Proven over time.

BTG, the intellectual property and technology commercialisation company, has been creating major products in the health and high tech sectors for more than 50 years. Our proven track record in creating commercial success from inventions speaks for itself and includes:

- *Magnetic Resonance Imaging* — the first MRI manufacturing licences were secured in 1983; since then, BTG has licensed every major MRI manufacturer

- *Multilevel Cell Memory* — enables storage of multiple bits of information in a single memory cell, thereby at least doubling the storage capacity of memory devices

- *Campath®* — the first humanised monoclonal antibody for use as a treatment for patients with B-cell chronic lymphocytic leukaemia

- *BeneFIX®* — recombinant Factor IX for the treatment of Haemophilia B

- *Tomudex™* — cytotoxic agent used in the treatment of colorectal cancer

BTG creates value by investing in intellectual property and technology development, and in early stage ventures. We realise value through technology licensing, patent assertion and disposal of equity investments.

BTG has a strong portfolio of over 240 technologies across a broad range of technology sectors, with a particular focus on oncology, ageing & neuroscience, molecular diagnostics & life science enabling technologies, semiconductors and optoelectronics.

———————

Please contact us through our website for further information on our portfolio and the technology areas where we are searching for new ideas.

www.btgplc.com

a handbook of
intellectual
property
management

a handbook of
intellectual
property
management

Protecting, developing and exploiting your IP assets

consultant editors
ADAM JOLLY & JEREMY PHILPOTT

published in association with
THE PATENT OFFICE

London and Stering, VA

Publisher's note

This information is current as of April 2004. Every possible effort has been made to ensure that the information contained in this book is accurate at the time of going to press, and the publishers and authors cannot accept responsibility for any errors or omissions, however caused. No responsibility for loss or damage occasioned to any person acting, or refraining from action, as a result of the material in this publication can be accepted by the editors, the publisher or any of the authors.

First published in Great Britain and the United States in 2004 by Kogan Page Limited.

120 Pentonville Road
London N1 9JN
United Kingdom
www.kogan-page.co.uk

22883 Quicksilver Drive
Sterling VA 20166-2012
USA

© Kogan Page and Contributors, 2004

The right of Jeremy Philpott and Adam Jolly to be identified as the authors of this work has been asserted by them in accordance with the Copyright, Designs and Patents Act 1988.

The views expressed in this book are those of the author, and are not necessarily the same as those of the Patent Office.

ISBN 0 7494 4223 9

British Library Cataloguing-in-Publication Data

A CIP record for this book is available from the British Library.

Library of Congress Cataloging-in-Publication Data

A handbook of intellectual property management : protecting, developing and exploiting your IP assets / consultant editors, Jeremy Philpott and Adam Jolly.
    p. cm.
  Includes index
  ISBN 0-7494-4223-9
  1. Intellectual property. 2. Intellectual capital--Management. 3. Technological innovation--Management. I. Philpott, Jeremy. II. Jolly, Adam.
  K1401.H36 2004
  346.04'8--dc22
                   2004015100

Typeset by Saxon Graphics Ltd, Derby
Printed and bound in Great Britain by Thanet Press Ltd, Margate

MewburnEllis
— LLP —

Mewburn Ellis LLP is one of the UK's largest firms of Chartered Patent Attorneys, European Patent Attorneys, European Trade Mark Attorneys and European Design Attorneys, with offices in London, Manchester, Cambridge and Bristol.

We handle the full range of intellectual property issues: patents, trade marks, designs, industrial copyright and related matters. Our attorneys will help you with all intellectual property matters, such as:

- Preparing and filing applications for patents, trade marks and designs

- Registration of patents, trade marks and designs in the UK and abroad

- Searches

- Computerised renewals service

- Patents expertise in all technical fields

- Specialised trade marks department

- In-house specialist lawyers handling licensing, transfers and litigation support

A large number of free detailed information sheets on most topics of interest can be found on our website, www.mewburn.com

For further information, please contact us at: mail@mewburn.com, or your preferred local office:

York House 23 Kingsway London WC26 6HP	Bridgewater House Whitworth Street Manchester M1 6LT	Newnham House Cambridge Business Park Cambridge CB4 0WZ	No.1 Redcliff Street Bristol BS1 6NP
Tel: 020 7240 4405 Fax: 020 7240 9339	Tel: 0161 247 7722 Fax: 0161 247 7766	Tel: 01223 420383 Fax: 01223 423792	Tel: 0117 926 6411 Fax: 0117 926 5692

IP excellence. Commercial relevance.

BTG, the intellectual property (IP) and technology commercialisation company, applies IP and commercial expertise, together with specialist skills in science and technology, to create major products in the health and high tech sectors.

Our team of patent attorneys have proven skills in the creation, development, enrichment, protection and assertion of patents. Their pragmatic approach, working in multidisciplinary teams alongside market professionals and science & technology experts, ensures the commercial relevance of the patents BTG looks after.

Our reputation is built on our in-house ability to:

- construct optimised, robust patent portfolios

- provide worldwide patent coverage

- extend and enhance patents through technology bundling and post grant procedures

- assert patents through litigation and arbitration

- assess scope and then audit patent licences

BTG currently manages around 3800 patents covering more than 240 technologies.

Please contact us through our website if you would like to hear more about how BTG uniquely combines patent, market and technology expertise to deliver value in the health and high tech sectors.

www.btgplc.com BTG

Contents

Keeping a Sharp Eye on your Patents

Bristows' lawyers see patents from their clients' perspective: as a vital lever to business success. As a law firm dedicated to serving businesses with interests in intellectual property and technology, we work closely with our clients to protect their intellectual property rights in industry sectors ranging from pharmaceuticals, electronics, IT and telecommunications to consumer products, television and entertainment. Described as "brilliant" by clients and relied upon to be "incredibly thorough at all times", Bristows has a strong and long established client base in Europe, the USA and Japan.

Bristows has an unrivalled team of 80 lawyers specialising in patents and other intellectual property. With over 160 years of experience in the patent field, the firm has earned an international reputation as a leading IP law firm and has developed one of the largest IP practices in Europe; yet remains a friendly niche firm compatible with the needs of growing and new companies.

Lawyers for **Businesses**
that **Create** and **Innovate**

www.bristows.com

Urquhart-Dykes & Lord LLP

Urquhart-Dykes & Lord is one of the UK's leading patent
and trade mark practices, being consistently ranked in
the top tier of providers in the Legal 500 review.
We have a network of offices throughout the UK and
specialist attorney teams focusing on all major areas
of technology, and on trade marks.
We are highly client orientated and take a proactive
interest in our client's business.
We aim to become integral to the decision
making process of our clients.

For further information please contact one
of the following offices:

30 WELBECK STREET, LONDON W1G 8ER
T +44 (0) 20 7487 1550 | F +44 (0) 20 7487 1599

TOWER NORTH CENTRAL, MERRION WAY, LEEDS LS2 8PA
T +44 (0) 113 245 2388 | F +44 (0) 113 243 0446

THREE TRINITY COURT, 21-27 NEWPORT ROAD, CARDIFF CF24 0AA
T +44 (0) 29 20487993 | F +44 (0) 29 20488016

MIDSUMMER HOUSE, 413 MIDSUMMER BOULEVARD, MILTON KEYNES MK9 3BN
T +44 (0) 1908 666645 | F +44 (0) 1908 351155

ST. NICHOLAS CHAMBERS, AMEN CORNER, NEWCASTLE UPON TYNE NE1 1PE
T +44 (0) 191 261 8573 | F +44 (0) 191 222 1604

NEW PRIESTGATE HOUSE, 57 PRIESTGATE, PETERBOROUGH PE1 1JX
T +44 (0) 1733 340011 | F +44 (0) 1733 566387

ALEXANDRA HOUSE, 1 ALEXANDRA ROAD, SWANSEA SA1 5ED
T +44 (0) 1792 474327 | F +44 (0) 1792 458244

Web: www.udl.co.uk
Email: email@udl.co.uk

Foreword

Just having this book puts your business ahead of many others. The number of businessmen and women who know nothing about even the basics of intellectual property (IP) is truly frightening. Too many businesses build reputations without protecting their brands. Too many businesses invest in costly R&D when cheaper technical solutions could have been licensed-in or read from a patent database for free. Too many businesses let others run away with their creative material, unaware that they have copyrights they can invoke; or they unwittingly infringe the copyrights of others.

Those who know how to lever their creative potential to best effect in the market place are in the minority – but they are running rings around everyone else.

For some time we have had an information-led economy, where trading in knowledge and communication has outpaced trade in conventional tangible 'things'. But the new economy goes beyond that, into the intangible realm of ideas. Innovation is the buzzword in business and government today, because those who innovate are those who stay ahead of their competitors.

The variety of IP rights, and the different ways in which they work, can be bewildering at first. But even a basic grasp of some of the key issues can mean the difference between success and failure.

The broad range of expert opinions in this book means that there is something for everyone here. Take the authors' advice as the starting point to finding out more about the IP rights that matter most to your business, be it copyright in your software, databases, artwork or music; trade marks for your emerging brands; design rights for your products and their packaging; or patents for the new technology in your products or processes.

Your business ventures prosper when you can minimize risk and maximize opportunities. IP presents both – it is up to you to understand the pitfalls and trophies in your own IP landscape and get the best deal for yourself. Good luck!

Ron Marchant
Chief Executive
The Patent Office

1
Establishing rights

Why intellectual property matters

Intellectual property is at the heart of competitive strategy, argues Ian Harvey, CEO of BTG, the intellectual property and technology commercialization company.

Today, intellectual property (IP) underpins between 50 and 70 per cent of a country's private sector gross domestic product (GDP), so it is often the difference between commercial success and failure. Because we now operate in a global village, when anything can be produced almost anywhere with instant communication, what you own is what you have thought about, created and designed. It is inevitable that the core of a company will become its intellectual capacity.

That intellectual output is protected by formal intellectual property rights. Patents, trade marks and copyright are powerful competitive advantages, because individuals and corporations own them and can enforce them in the courts. Other competitive advantages are less durable: first to market is easily eroded; price is open to attack; and design is easily lost.

It is striking how few senior managers really understand what intellectual property can do for them. Even in technology companies, many chairman and chief executive officers (CEOs) do not grasp the simple distinction in patents between patentability and freedom to use. It is like not knowing the difference between profit and cash flow. You do not have to be an accountant to be a chairman or CEO, but you have to understand the fundamentals, so you can ask the right questions. A patent gives its owner the right to stop others from using an invention. It does not give the owner the right to use the invention itself – a subtle but vital distinction. And if executives do not fully grasp that a patent is just a 'keep off the grass' sign, how are they going to raise more sophisticated points about using IP as a strategic tool?

Managers must understand that IP is a live asset that needs to be managed like any other asset. It is going to be challenged, so organizations need the resources to rebut those challenges. In the United States, executives clearly understand what is happening in IP. They use it (sometimes abuse it) and debate it. Elsewhere IP has a more ambiguous status. But to think it does not matter is a wasted opportunity. We operate in a set of global IP systems. If we are going to succeed, we had better use them to maximum advantage. If we do not, everyone else will. You have to understand what the global IP system can do for you.

In fact, very few companies integrate IP and corporate strategy properly. There are exceptions, such as IBM and the majority of the pharmaceuticals industry. For IBM the headline figure is that IP generates US $1.5 billion a year in royalties. What is more important is how organizations think through their product strategy. Where is the IP going to come from? Should they license their competitors? Do they develop and sell the technology them-selves, or buy it in?

So, for instance, IBM licensed its leading-edge liquid crystal display technology to a former competitor in Taiwan. Having low-cost high-quality first production, as well as generating revenue from all its competitors, was a better commercial proposition for IBM than producing screens itself. Such a strategy depends on understanding what IP the organization has, finding an edge and deciding whether to invent or buy technology. Most companies are nowhere near this position. It takes between 5 and 10 years to evolve to where an organization is really operating at full IP throttle.

For example, IP is often scattered throughout a company. No one knows who owns it. No one knows what is there. Yet it is viewed as the crown jewels. The thought of licensing it out is unthinkable, when in fact it might be the best thing to do.

Too often patents are filed just because an invention has been made. Why exactly does the organization need one?

- Is it to keep competitors out of the market, or is it to license competitors to generate revenues?
- Is it to build a portfolio?
- Does the organization want to combine it with other technologies?
- Does the organization make narrow filings of patents so it can defend them more easily?
- Does the organization have more limited resources, and is it thinking about broader applications?

Once a patent has been granted, the next question is how it should be reinforced with trade marks. And for organizations in the copyright industry, where technology is moving extraordinarily quickly in the digital world, how can they adapt and take advantage? They do not want to find themselves defending a position from 20 years ago when the rest of the world has moved on. It is a question of understanding how to use technology, trade marks and copyright to be commercially effective in a rapidly changing environment. Those who will win are those who understand where the IP landscape is going. What can be defended and what cannot?

How to then build a portfolio depends on its objectives. In pharmaceuticals, it is important to have strong rights to a new chemical entity which the company alone can sell. In electronics, companies are selling complex pieces of equipment, which makes it likely that patents from outside the organization will be involved. If there is to be freedom to use, there may well be cross-licensing, so the company has the right to sell its product even though it is using someone else's patented technology.

A decade ago, cross-licensing for no value was commonplace. Today, people are looking more closely at the value of each portfolio. There have been instances where companies have lost hundreds of millions of dollars in revenue because they did not understand the value of what they had. It might be a case of a subsidiary unwittingly licensing patents held by other parts of the company. This is a prime example of a situation where patents need to be held centrally, so they are corporate assets and the company decides how they are to be used to create shareholder value.

Another decision is whether to strengthen a portfolio by acquiring or selling rights. This is a complex market. Like an Old Master painting, the value of IP is hard to establish and depends on the buyer. Auctions are not generally suitable: they work better when what is being sold is an easily defined object with clear rights. Most IP is more complicated that that. So when an organization is selling IP, it should look towards people or organizations to whom it will be very valuable. Revenues from IP licences are almost as predictable as an annuity stream, with a high certainty of revenue for many years, unless the whole industry changes.

Some IP rights have a time and a place. Some never work, because complementary technologies do not yet exist to make them possible. So it is better to have a number of different products, because it is hard to predict which one is going to win. BTG aims to have 15–20 per cent of IP on its books, for which it does not know what the commercial application is going to be, but thinks it is really good technology which could be transformational. Its time has not yet come, although the organization reviews this every year.

Do not pin your hopes just on finding lost treasure in the attic. The fundamental question is how to use IP as a core strategy, and how to use it to greatest advantage. That is where the real long-term value lies. Selling for value is important, but putting it at the heart of a corporate strategy is the big prize.

Ian Harvey is the CEO of BTG plc, the IP and technology commercialization company. He is chair of the UK government's Intellectual Property Advisory Committee. He became a director of the UK's Intellectual Property Institute in 1998 and its chair in 1999.

BTG creates value by investing in intellectual property and technology development, and in early stage ventures. It realizes value through technology licensing, patent assertion and disposal of equity investments. Through a multidisciplinary approach, it applies intellectual property and commercial expertise, together with specialist skills in science and technology, to create major product opportunities in the health and high-tech sectors. BTG has commercialized important innovations, including magnetic resonance imaging, multilevel cell (MLC) memory, and Factor IX blood clotting protein, the first recombinant treatment for Haemophilia B. BTG operates through wholly owned subsidiaries BTG International Ltd and BTG International Inc in the UK and United States respectively. Further information about BTG can be found at www.btgplc.com

ABLETT & STEBBING

Providing patent, design and
trademark protection around the world.

Ablett & Stebbing
Caparo House
101-103 Baker Street
London W1U 6FQ
Tel: +44 (0) 207 935 7720
Fax: +44 (0) 207 935 7790
www.absteb.co.uk

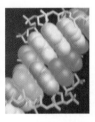

Innovative ideas frequently form one of the core assets of a business. Typically, they are based around one or more of, for example, inventions, trade marks, designs or know how. All too often, such assets are left unprotected or unrecognised, which in the long term leaves the business both weak and vulnerable to conflict with similar assets of another business.

As patent and trade mark attorneys, we specialise in advising exclusively on those areas of the law relating to these assets and in identifying and obtaining appropriate intellectual property rights for them. In addition, it is our aim to provide a service of the highest quality at a reasonable cost.

We believe that we are able to offer this through careful selection, training and supervision of our staff, together with the development and investment in uniquely efficient office systems.

Our Clients include:

Aberdeen University
Alcoa (CSI) Europe Limited
Alza Corporation
C R Bard Inc
Manolo Blahnik
Marks Barfield Architects
Pentax Corporation
Rhino Linings USA Inc
USB Warburg
W S Atkins Limited
Wyeth

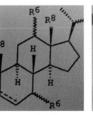

As a result, since the founders of the firm started in business in 1988, we have progressively expanded to now represent a diverse range of clients from all parts of the world, varying from small enterprises, Universities, and major companies in Europe, Japan and the United States of America.

Lloyd Wise
Commonwealth House
1-19 New Oxford Street
London WC1A 1LW

Tel: +44 (0) 20 7571 6200
Fax: +44 (0) 20 7571 6250
london@lloydwise.co.uk
www.lloydwise.com

Lloyd Wise

**Lloyd Wise,
McNeight & Lawrence**
Highbank House
Exchange Street
Stockport SK3 0ET

Tel: +44 (0) 161 480 6394
Fax: +44 (0) 161 480 2622
manchester@lloydwise.co.uk
www.lloydwise.com

Get an outline of Intellectual Property laws in Lloyd Wise specialist countries

Peruse our FAQ – We have one of the most comprehensive sets of answers to FAQ in the industry

Find filing requirements and timelines for filing and prosecuting new applications in Lloyd Wise specialist countries

Send us an online inquiry or online instructions for filing trade mark applications

Download relevant forms

www.lloydwise.com

Meet our attorney

View our interactive chronology

Read papers on changes in law and topics of interest in Lloyd Wise specialist countries

Find full directions to all our offices including real time flight information

Link to sites for trade mark, patent & design searching on the Internet and to official bodies and treaties/ conventions

Lloyd Wise & Co
4005-4007 Tower Two
Lippo Centre
89 Queensway
Central
Hong Kong

Tel: (+852) 2526 5654
Fax: (+852) 2868 5438
mail@lloydwise.com.hk
www.lloydwise.com

利
衛

Lloyd Wise
200 Cantonment Road
#14-01 Southpoint
Singapore 089763

Tel: (+65) 6227 8986
Fax: (+65) 6227 3898
mail@lloydwise.com.sg
www.lloydwise.com

Which rights apply?

A number of different rights may apply to innovations in products, processes and services, says Chris Vigars at Haseltine Lake.

There are many different kinds of innovation: big and small, revolutionary and evolutionary, practical and artistic, technical and intellectual. The one thing that all kinds of innovation have in common is that they can potentially be protected using intellectual property (IP) rights.

Several different kinds of IP right are available, each of which has individual characteristics, advantages and disadvantages. Registered IP rights are secured through registration procedures with the appropriate authorities, and include patents, trade marks and registered designs. Unregistered IP rights, such as copyright and design right, exist automatically, but tend to be more limited than registered rights. These rights will be discussed in greater detail elsewhere, but their main characteristics are summarized below.

Patents are concerned with protecting technological inventions. Such inventions typically provide advantages over existing technology. A patentable invention usually exists where a technical problem has been overcome, or where an innovative material, product or process has been developed. As is discussed in more detail elsewhere, to be patentable an invention must be new, involve an inventive step, and be industrially applicable. It is important not to overestimate the size of the inventive step required to secure patent protection for an invention. Also, it can be advantageous to obtain broad patent protection outside the immediate application of the invention. Such broad protection can lead to licensing opportunities, and hence revenue, in non-core areas.

Registered trade marks (RTMs) deal with branding of products and services, and normally involve the registration of a name or logo in respect of certain classes of goods and services. It is possible to register some three-dimensional and non-visual trade marks as well as names and logos. In order to obtain a registration, the trade mark must be distinctive, and not descriptive of the products or services to which it will be applied.

Registered designs protect appearance. Two-dimensional surface decoration, the three-dimensional shape of an article, computer icons, packaging, and typefaces can all be protected by registered designs. Registered designs are concerned only with appearance and not with function. For registration, a design must be new and have an individual character which sets the design apart from existing similar designs.

Copyright has the advantage that it exists automatically for original creations in the artistic, musical, literary or dramatic arts. Copyright enables the owner of the right to take action against someone who has copied the creation. However, copyright is limited because in order to prove infringement it is necessary to show actual copying of the creation. This is in contrast to the registered rights mentioned above, where independent creation can be the subject of an infringement action.

Unregistered design right is similar to copyright in that it exists automatically, and that there is a need to prove actual copying in order to show infringement. Broadly speaking, design right serves to protect specific features of the shape of an article, as will be discussed in more detail elsewhere.

It will be clear that a particular innovation may be protected by more than one IP right. Relying on a 'web' of various rights, each of which protects a different aspect, provides a robust form of defence against competitors. The protection gained should be effective and enforceable, and the cost of obtaining such protection must be balanced against the value of the idea being protected. The different rights that could be available for products, processes and services are discussed below.

Protecting a new product

The technical detail of the product, that is those details that give the new product functional or structural advantages over similar existing products, can be protected using patents. Technical details suitable for patent protection include the materials from which the product is constructed, the method of construction, and the devices and components included in the product. Typically, a new product will feature a range of innovations that can be protected using patents. There will, therefore, often be a number of patents associated with a new product.

The appearance of the product can be protected using registered design, copyright, and unregistered design right. The aspects of a product's appearance suitable for design registration include distinctive overall shape, and surface patterning.

The branding of the product can be protected using one or more registered trade marks. The product and model name, and the supplier's name or brand, can be protected in this way.

Protecting a new process

A process is a method for performing a task. For example, a method for manufacturing devices, components or products, a method for handling data processing, and a method of operating a product all come under the umbrella term 'process'. For manufacturing processes and data processing, the novel aspects of the process can be patented. For example, a new robotic painting technique for the automotive industry, or a method for processing video data signals, could be the subject of a patent. To qualify for patent protection, a process should have some technical character, and should not relate only to abstract ideas, such as business or mathematical methods.

If the process can be used as a marketing tool, then registering the name of the process as a registered trade mark could be considered.

Protecting a new service

New services are generally business-related ideas, and are more abstract than the processes described above. For this reason, trade mark registration and confidentiality should be relied upon. Branding a new service can often be the most effective way to protect the service, by distinguishing it in the consumer's mind from similar services of other providers.

Example IP Strategy

That is the theory. Below are a realistic example of a new product, and suggestions for an IP strategy to protect the product.

Consider a new mobile telephone, to be sold under a new brand name. The developers have spent a lot of effort improving the antenna of the telephone to improve its sensitivity, and have designed a new combined display and keypad. The telephone also handles incoming calls in a new way that can conserve battery power. The telephone is constructed from an entirely new, super-light material, which has been developed specifically for the purpose, but which could be used for a variety of consumer electronics devices. A new manufacturing technique has also been developed in order to minimize wastage of the new material.

The IP strategy should aim to cover as many different aspects of the protection of the new telephone as possible. Since a mobile telephone is a relatively high-value product, with wide appeal, then the costs of obtaining the full range of registered IP rights will be justified. Naturally, other products and processes may benefit from a more limited use of registered IP rights.

For this new mobile telephone, the new brand name and model name will be important to distinguish it in an already crowded market place. Protecting the brand name and model name using RTMs should therefore be considered.

A major selling point for a mobile telephone is the way it looks. Design registration should be sought for the overall look of the telephone, as well as for some of the more significant parts. In addition, any new icons that are used on the display may be protected by registered design.

Another major selling point of the new telephone will be its technical advantages over its rivals. In the example, the improved antenna, the combined display and keypad, the call handling techniques, and new manufacturing processes should be the subject of patent applications.

The innovative material should also be the subject of a patent application, which is directed to the material itself, rather than to its use in a mobile telephone. Since the material has a wide range of potential applications, broad protection should be sought to provide the opportunity for alternative sources of revenue through licensing outside of the mobile telephone market.

Chris Vigars joined Haseltine Lake in October 1993, after gaining an engineering science Honours degree from St Edmund Hall, Oxford University. He qualified as a British Chartered Patent Attorney and European Patent Attorney in 1997, and has been a partner at Haseltine Lake since May 2000. Chris is experienced in all aspects of drafting and prosecuting patent applications in many jurisdictions around the world. He specializes in electrical and electronic inventions. For further information contact cvigars@haseltinelake.com

electrical trademarks
mechanical chemistry engineering
electronics

Brookes Batchellor LLP
a new name in British Intellectual Property

The UK patent attorney firms of Brookes & Martin and Batchellor, Kirk & Co merged their resources in 2001 to create the new partnership of Brookes Batchellor. The new firm operates as Patent and Trade Mark attorneys from offices conveniently located in central London close to Farringdon Station (Metropolitan Line and Thameslink), and at Royal Tunbridge Wells in Kent, with its easy access to the UK motorway network, London's Gatwick Airport and the Channel Tunnel.

Brookes Batchellor advises its British and international clients on all aspects of Intellectual Property. The patent attorneys of the firm have expertise in all the major technical fields including pharmaceuticals, chemistry, electronics, electrical and mechanical engineering.

The firm routinely files and processes patent applications at the European Patent Office; at the UK Patent Office; and for countries throughout the world, directly or under the PCT (Patent Co-operation Treaty), using long established relationships with local Attorneys in the relevant countries. Also the firm files and processes applications to register trademarks at the UK Trade Mark Office; at the European Community Trademark Office; internationally under the Madrid Protocol; and worldwide in cooperation with local Attorneys. We also deal with UK Design Registrations and Community Designs.

Although in numerical terms most patent activity is derived from large international organisations, the firm recognises that inventions from smaller groups - even individuals - can become of major importance, with associated commercial success. Whether acting for a larger or smaller client, work will be handled on an individual basis, and dealt with by a named person to the highest professional and technical standards. The firm's aim is, not just to follow instructions given, but to be pro-active and make suggestions to maximise the benefit our clients are receiving.

Brookes Batchellor's mission is to approach the process of protecting clients' intellectual property with the same degree of enthusiasm and commitment as the original inventors.

Hard rights versus soft rights

Some IP rights arise automatically; some have to be registered. Some are easily enforced; others require a mountain of evidence. Dr Jeremy Philpott of the Patent Office explains how different rights apply in practice.

Intellectual property (IP) law encompasses a variety of rights that protect creativity in its myriad forms with different remedies. Knowing what is protected by each right, and what is required to employ each right, is crucial to any business, innovator or artisan.

An easy way to distinguish the rights from each other is to recognize those that are 'hard' and those that are 'soft'. (See Table 1.3.1.) For those who like something for nothing, the 'soft' rights appeal. These require no registration, no fees and no formalities for rights to arise. Chief among these is copyright, which is free and automatic as soon as any original musical, dramatic, literary or artistic work is created. These four classes for copyright protection can spread as wide as film, television, radio, Web sites, photographs and software. Similar protection extends to such things as databases, although the rights against extraction and reutilization of the data therein last only 15 years from creation or publication. True copyright for (for example) an original song, painting or play lasts for the lifetime of the author, plus a further 70 years.

It is as well that the rights in such things arise automatically – what photographer would have the time to formally register the copyright in each

Table 1.3.1 Hard and soft IPR

'Soft' IPR	'Hard' IPR (aka 'industrial property')
Copyright	
Database rights	
Unregistered design rights	Registered designs
Unregistered trade marks™	***Registered trade marks®***
Trade secrets, confidential information	Patents

and every shot he or she prints? Unregistered design right needs no explanation, and protects the external appearance of articles, be they artistic or functional. Unregistered trade marks often provide businesses, especially retailers, with protection in their good name and the reputation vested in their brand for many years – and they do not even realize it.

As any business grows it will develop a body of proprietary information, much of which is critical to its success, and valuable to its competitors. You only need to ask yourself, 'Would this information harm us if leaked or lost, or benefit competitors if it was in their hands?' and you will soon realize just how many trade secrets your organization owns. Would a competitor not love to have a copy of the customer list? Like a genie out of a bottle, once these secrets are out the organization will never be able to get them back. Has the marketing team blabbed about a new project in making promises to customers? Suppliers might engage in idle chatter with their other customers (your organization's competitors) about what unusual raw materials your organization is now ordering. Contractors and staff who have left might now be working for the opposition; consultants know all the company's weaknesses and might now be coaching its competitors. Can any organization put a price on staff whose familiarity ('know-how') with its unique processes means that they are more productive than any replacement could hope to be?

If the thought of all these 'soft' rights sounds too good to be true, there is a fly in the ointment. In life you only get what you pay for, and in the case of the 'soft' rights the organization will have paid nothing to acquire them. This means that if it is placed in the unfortunate position of needing to assert its rights against an infringer, it will have an evidential hill to climb before it can make a case stick in court. Does the right that it is claimed is infringed actually exist, and if it does, to whom does it belong? If creative work is produced in the course of employment, copyright in it normally belongs to the employer. Conversely, if a company has paid a contractor handsomely to create some artwork or software, but neglected to acquire copyright in the contractor's work, the contractor will retain ownership and be entitled to demand additional fees if the company copies or adapts the work. The assumption that anyone owns the copyright in what he or she consider to be his/her creation can be misplaced, and having that assumption corrected in court can be expensive!

Take for example the dispute between knitwear designer Shirin Guild and her erstwhile business partner Eskandar Nabavi. After their business relationship ended, Mr Nabavi continued to design similar knitwear, and instructed a manufacturer, Havelock, to make his articles. Mrs Guild sued Mr Nabavi for copyright infringement. The court did not believe knitwear qualified for copyright protection as it was not a musical, dramatic, literary or artistic work. Mrs Guild countered that her designs were works of 'artistic craftsmanship', and hence qualified for copyright protection. Not so, said the court: the act of mass production (even on a limited scale) meant that the clothing had forfeited copyright protection and qualified only for design protection. In the absence of a registration, Mrs Guild had to fall back on unregistered design right, under which she was powerless to prevent Mr Nabavi or Havelock from making the knitwear if they paid her royalties.

On appeal it got even worse for Mrs Guild. The appeal court decided that as her designs were based on old Iranian peasant clothing they lacked originality and hence were not deserving of protection at all! Even if differences between the modern knitwear and the old traditional clothing that it echoed could confer 'originality' on the designs, it was not at all clear that Mrs Guild was the sole creator, given the creative input of Mr Nabavi and staff at Havelock.

(The case in question is *Guild v Eskandar* [2001] FSR 38 p645, further appealed as *Eskandar Nabavi v Eskandar Ltd and Shirin Guild* [2002] IPLR 6 [2002], EWCA Civ 316, Court of Appeal.)

No such uncertainty with the 'hard' rights. The fact that there is an entry on a register, which describes the nature of the right and lists the name of the owner(s), means that no question about the existence or ownership of the right can arise. A further advantage is that the 'hard' rights give remedies even where the alleged infringer bleats, 'But what I have done is a coincidence, I never copied from you!' Ignorance of another's registered rights will never get someone off the hook, which is all the more reason to check registers of trade marks and databases of patents at regular intervals. Conversely, to make an allegation of infringement stick with regard to a 'soft' right like copyright, it is necessary to *prove* copying – that the infringing product post-dates, and has its genesis in, the original. Faced with a defence of 'But I made mine first – it's yours that is the copy!' or 'It's a coincidence!', the organization has to bring the necessary evidence to convince a court that its rights are really being infringed.

Just because a right is displayed on a register it does not make it absolute. Ownership disputes can break out occasionally, just as they would over any other type of property, especially when companies merge, dissolve, are sold or liquidated. Despite registration, trade marks can become unenforceable if they are not used in the market place for a period of five years or more (for instance, if a later trader adopts or recycles another's defunct mark, there might be no infringement). Patents can be rendered invalid, most usually if the invention is shown not to be as new as was first believed when the patent was granted. The demise of a patent after grant is thankfully a very rare event, because certainty is what underpins the patent system. But no patent office can be said to know about every invention or disclosure ever made, so when it grants a patent for an invention in good faith, there is always a chance that at a later date a witness will come forward with evidence which shows that prior to the patent's filing date, the same or a similar invention was in the public domain. This would even include the patentee's disclosure of the invention prior to patent filing, if he or she did so without an obligation of confidence.

You might come across the term 'industrial property' which, unhelpfully, has the same initials as 'intellectual property'. The former is the antique term for the registrable or 'hard' rights, whereas the latter term encompasses both 'hard' and 'soft' rights. More detailed explanation of the nature of all of these rights appears in Part 5.

It is also worth noting that Table 1.3.1 shows (in bold italics) the only two IP rights for which criminal sanctions are available in addition to the civil remedies. The criminal sanctions of fines or imprisonment are provided for wilful and commercially damaging infringements of copyright material ('piracy') and registered trade marked goods ('counterfeiting'). Prosecutions are often brought by trading standards officers or the police, rather than the rights owners, against criminal gangs manufacturing and selling pirated computer games and software, pirate music and films, counterfeit clothing, fake cosmetics and the like. (These issues are discussed in more detail in Part 6.)

Commercial disputes in relation to copyright and registered trade marks are resolved using civil law remedies, primarily injunctions and damages. It is important to remember that for registered designs and patents the civil sanctions are the only remedies available for infringement. No one ever went to prison for infringing a patent!

This book does not cover the *sui generis* rights which are offshoots of modern IP law. Such rights are related, but of interest only to narrow market sectors. For example, there is a short-lived 'soft' right for semiconductor topographies, similar to an unregistered design right. For plant breeders seeking to protect their investment in R&D there is a 'hard' *sui generis* 'plant varieties right' which is similar to a patent. In a way analogous to trade mark law, producers whose foods or drinks bear a place name that has become synonymous with the kind, type or quality of the goods (Parma ham, Champagne, Camembert cheese and the like) can acquire protection through a 'protected geographical indication' (PGI). Once a specification is registered describing what qualities a product must have to be allowed to bear the place name in the PGI (for example, the type of processing and location), any product meeting that specification is entitled to use the PGI.

Just one parting thought – seatbelts do not prevent car accidents, they only protect people in the event of disaster. So it is with IP rights. Most of the time the fact that an individual or organization possesses them will not seem to make any difference, but in the event of a crisis (infringement) they are the difference between potentially crippling financial loss and the protection of anyone's dearest asset: their creativity.

Jeremy Philpott joined the Patent Office in 1996 as a patent examiner, and moved to marketing in 2000. For the last three years he has handled the Patent Office's PR brief.

Jeremy raises awareness and understanding of the Patent Office and of IP through his media work, regularly giving interviews on radio, television and to the press. He has been acting as an IP advisor to the producers of the increasing number of television and radio shows about inventions or IP. He works closely with the Patent Office's PR agency to develop media campaigns and exploit opportunities as they arise in the press. Wherever an IP story breaks in the media, or there is a consultation to publicize, Jeremy is always on hand to explain the issues and clarify the law.

For more information about any aspect of IP visit www.patent.gov.uk or call 08459 500 505.

Two versions of IP: EU and US

Dr John Collins of Marks & Clerk highlights some fundamental differences between IP practice in the European Union and the United States.

The EU and the United States are two of the most commercially important markets in the world. Although built on the same concepts, the intellectual property systems of the EU and the United States have evolved to create some fundamental differences between the two. An intellectual property (IP) owner can only realize the full potential of IP assets through an understanding and respect of these variations.

Patents

Patent protection for inventions is available in the EU via two different routes – national patents administered by national patent offices, and European patents administered by the European Patent Office (EPO), which is based in Munich. Although procedures vary between national offices, the substantive law is aligned with the EPO. Although European patents are granted centrally by the EPO, they comprise a 'bundle' of national patents. That the EU currently has no unitary patent system is a major source of debate and consultation that has been carrying on for years. While a framework has now been agreed there are still obstacles and patent owners will have to wait until the next decade until an unitary system is likely to be operational.

Patent law in Europe is based on a '*first to file*' principle, wherein the person entitled to a patent for an invention is the first person to file the patent application. However, the US patent system is based on a '*first to invent*' system. So if two people have filed patent applications for the same invention, evidence such as inventors' notebooks is submitted to determine who derived the invention first. The keeping of notebooks and invention records by inventors can therefore prove essential, and is a practice that should be observed by anyone looking to register a patent in the United States.

Under EU law a patent application must be filed before any public disclosure of the invention. However, under US law a patent application can be filed up to 12 months after disclosure of the invention by the inventor. This fall-back position can be useful if an inventor has inadvertently disclosed the invention before a patent was filed. At least valid patent protection in the United States can be obtained even if EU protection is lost. In general, inventors must think whether patent protection is required well in advance of disclosure, to give enough time for the preparation and filing of a patent application.

The United States is much more liberal than the EU when it comes to stipulating what can and cannot be patented. One key area is medical and surgical methods. The EU specifically prohibits the patenting of medical and surgical techniques whereas the United States has no such limitation. Another key area is business methods. The EU only allows patents to be granted for inventions that are a '*technical solution to a technical problem*'. In contrast, the United States allows patents to anything '*new and useful*', and thus patents for pure business methods are allowed. This is a major difference in the patent laws, and one that can have a significant commercial impact. Companies cannot ignore the possibility of protecting their business methods in the United States even if they are not protectable in the EU.

The procedures for obtaining patent protection in the United States are somewhat more arduous than those in the EU. The applicant and his or her representatives have a duty of good faith and candour to disclose in the patent specification the best mode of making the invention that is known to the inventor. No key steps or features can be left out. Also, publications, products and the like that might have some relevance to the validity of the patent – known as prior art – must be notified to the patent examiner. Failure to comply with either of these requirements can render the patent invalid. If patent protection is to be sought in the United States, applicants must be open with their advisors, disclose all relevant material about the invention and the prior art, and be prepared to be patient!

Trade marks

Trade mark protection can be obtained in the EU as a unitary EU trade mark registration or as an individual national trade mark registration. In the EU, trade marks can be registered on the basis of an intention to use the mark when no actual use of it in the EU has yet taken place. The registration can be attacked on the basis of non-use only when the mark has not been used for a five-year period. In contrast, the US registration system is based on the requirement to use the mark in commerce in the United States before registration. Trade mark owners in Europe can circumvent this requirement by basing the US application for registration on a home registration in the EU. However, the renewal of the US registration requires a declaration by the proprietor of the mark that the mark has been used in commerce in the United States during the previous 10 years for the registered goods or services. If it has not been used for some goods or services, protection for these has to be surrendered. The effect of this is to keep the scope of US registrations narrower than in the EU, thus reducing the likelihood of potential infringement. Therefore, a strategy for trade mark registration is to seek broader speculative trade mark rights in the EU and more targeted trade mark rights in the United States.

Registered designs

IP rights in designs are registered in the United States as design patents (as opposed to utility patents for inventions), whereas in the EU designs can be registered as unitary EU registered designs or as separate national registered designs. Designs that can be registered are more restricted in the EU than in the United States, where almost any new design is registrable. In the EU a number of designs are excluded from protection, including designs that must fit with other parts (the 'must fit' exclusion), designs dictated solely by technical function, and designs that are not normally visible during use (for instance, interior parts). However, the protection afforded to EU designs is broader than that provided to US designs. In the EU protection extends to any article bearing the design, whereas in the United States the protection is limited to a claimed article bearing the design. Since the costs of obtaining EU design registration are very low, design owners are strongly recommended to make use of this registration procedure to protect their IP rights in their designs.

Copyright

In both the United States and the EU, copyright exists as soon as a copyright work is created. There is no requirement for registration to obtain this right. However, in the United States there is a copyright register, and before copyright is enforced it is a requirement that the copyright be registered at the Copyright Office (part of the US Patent and Trade Mark Office). There are also additional benefits to registering copyrights, which include the establishment of a copyright date and the right to statutory damages and attorneys' fees in certain circumstances.

IP enforcement

It is widely acknowledged that the cost of litigation in the United States is far higher than in the EU. There are also wide variations in the cost of litigation in the EU, since for patents and copyright there is no unitary EU, granting and enforcement system. National courts implement national procedures with their inherently different cost structures. In the EU, specialist courts and judges handle IP litigation. In contrast, in the United States IP litigation is handled by district courts with no specialist judges. In fact it is enshrined in the US Constitution that parties to litigation have the right to a jury trial. Thus, a jury will usually try even highly technical patent litigation. However, the damage awards in US litigation are very much larger than those in the EU, and attorneys who are prepared to work on a contingency fee basis are more prevalent.

Summary

There are many more pitfalls in obtaining and enforcing IP and particularly patents in the United States than in the EU. However, it has to be remembered that, in view of the market size of the United States, the potential benefits are high. The EU does not yet have truly uniform IP laws, and while there is continuous movement towards harmonization, it has been painfully slow. Until there is harmonization, the cost of obtaining patents across the EU will remain high. Even though the cost of enforcement of IP is generally lower in the EU than in the United States, the lack of unitary enforcement for patents and copyright imposes fragmented enforcement requirements on IP owners.

Dr John Collins is a partner at Marks & Clerk Patent and Trade Mark Attorneys, Europe's largest firm of intellectual property specialists. For further information contact: Jcollins@marks-clerk.com t: 020 7400 3000 www.marks-clerk.com

Brand equity

Intellectual property is an integral part of creating brand value, says David Haigh, CEO, Brand Finance plc.

The value of brands and trade marks

Brands can be sold, transferred or licensed, quite separately from the related product manufacturing capability. Although brands form a large part of the value of most organizations, a brand itself has no legal definition and is not the subject of a single identifiable right.

The visual identity of a brand incorporates its name, logo, get-up and design. Trade marks, copyright, design rights and common law can protect these factors. However, on their own they do not create the value of a brand. A brand's ability to generate earnings is a result of the values and attributes that consumers, employees and other stakeholders attach to the visual identity. This is often referred to as brand equity. These perceptions are created and nurtured by good management, skilful marketing and careful implementation.

A company can therefore own and protect certain aspects of a brand, but other factors reside in the minds of consumers. In reality, the benefits that can be derived from a brand 'follow' a transfer of ownership or the right to use the associated trade marks. It is not possible to separate the trade mark and other aspects of visual identity from the related consumer perceptions. This is reflected by the frequent use of the term 'the trade mark and associated goodwill' in licensing agreements.

The fact that a brand consists of more than just visual identity, or a label, is well illustrated by the different results between blind tasting and branded tasting of soft drinks. In blind tasting, Pepsi tends to outperform Coca-Cola. Once the brands are known, the preference is reversed. In instances such as this, the preference for one product over the other is clearly attributable to the perceptual components of the brand.

Brand preference creates value as a result of:

- premium prices;
- higher volumes;
- reduced volatility in earnings streams;
- new earnings streams through brand stretching;
- lower staff recruitment and retrenchment costs and the ability to attract high-quality recruits;
- better trade terms;
- lower finance costs.

Why value brands?

During the last decade, brand valuation has become a mainstream business tool, used for purposes including value-based marketing, merger and acquisition planning, and recognition of intangible assets on company balance sheets.

Marketing has traditionally operated independently from the rigorous financial evaluation that is used for other investments, and this situation still exists in many organizations. In a worst case scenario, it can result in bad decision making and poor company performance. Due to a growing realization of the importance of brands as value drivers, leading companies are increasing their understanding of how their brands impact on their business model. Financial analysis can then be used to estimate the expected and actual return on marketing investment. Value-based marketing techniques can also be used for the purpose of brand portfolio reviews, brand performance tracking and budget allocation.

Earnings, tax and borrowings

Trade marks are increasingly being licensed, both internally within large multinationals and to third parties. Brand valuation allows a realistic set of charges to be determined. These charges reflect the value of the asset being licensed. The primary benefit of a trade mark owner carrying out a detailed brand evaluation prior to entering into a licensing agreement is to ensure that full value is extracted from the agreement. An additional benefit in the case of internal licensing is that the brand evaluation supports the selected royalty rate for tax purposes.

As tax authorities have become aware of the increasing significance of brands and intangible assets in a company's wider valuation, both assessors and brand owners alike expect royalty rates to be paid or received where those intangible assets are used. Companies need to gauge how most effectively to gain value from their intangible assets while minimizing tax payments. The domicile of the brand needs to be carefully considered, as does the royalty rate charged for its use.

The continued recognition of brands as assets has increased the opportunity to use them to back specific borrowing lines. This is especially prevalent in the United States where companies like Disney have borrowed large sums against their brands.

Protection

There are some components of brands that lend themselves to different types of legal protection, namely names, symbols, logos and strap lines. Different forms of legal protection are available for each component. As a result, a brand owner must rely upon a mixture of trade mark, copyright, design right, common law and codes of practice for legal protection. These must be combined in order to be able to evaluate the level of legal protection enjoyed by a brand as a whole. Sub-categories such as colour, shape, sound and design must also be considered within each component.

Although a brand might include a number of protectable rights, trade marks are flexible commercial tools on which to base licensing and merchandising rights. Because trade marks have defined use classes, they lend themselves to clear definitions of rights by jurisdiction and product type.

Although a trade mark might not be registered in the UK, it does not mean that the unregistered mark has no protection. If the brand owner has established recognition in an unregistered name by use, to the extent that there is commercial goodwill arising from it, the owner is entitled to protect the goodwill at common law by an action in passing off.

Brand equity, the perceptions associated with the brand in the minds of consumers, is not entitled to legal protection. These perceptions are influenced every time the consumer has any contact with the brand, be it a direct experience with the product, advertising or other media exposure, an interaction with a representative of the brand or word of mouth. This component of a brand is 'owned' by the consumer. As a result the underlying equity of a brand, the aggregation of such perceptions, is constantly shifting.

The successful creation of brand value requires a combination of skills. IP has to be properly registered, controlled and protected. Skilful marketing is required to build and protect brand equity. Financial analysis informs the allocation of resources and tracking of brand performance. Tax planning is required to ensure that a tax-efficient structure is determined for legal and economic ownership of trade marks and transfer pricing.

In many organizations, these distinct skill sets reside in separate silos. The parties involved have different reporting lines and functional objectives that might not be aligned to those of the brand. This explains the many examples of dysfunctional brand behaviour. Examples include giving the rights to use valuable trade marks to joint ventures, or third parties, for little or no consideration; tax structures being ignored by operating companies; and brands being launched in markets without trade mark protection. The best solution to these issues is centralized brand ownership and management. The grouping of the required skills in a central, IP-focused company is the best method to facilitate effective brand management.

Conclusion

'Brands' are often said to be the most valuable assets of modern companies. Trade marks are the foundation and the legally transferable core of what is known as a 'brand'. It is these specific intangible assets that are increasingly being moved, traded and licensed. Central management of IP is a more efficient way of managing these powerful legal properties, and also offers strong tax advantages if well planned.

Beneath central IP management lies the ability to credibly value trade marks and associated goodwill for both capital and income tax purposes. Every IP practitioner should understand what is being valued and the means of valuation. Armed with this, practitioners will be in a position to control strategic decisions and generate significant value for their employers.

Brand Finance plc is the world's leading independent brand valuation consultancy. It advises strongly branded organizations, both large and small, on how to maximize shareholder value through effective brand management. Brand Finance now has a presence in eight countries, including Brazil, Hong Kong, Spain, the UK and the United States.

It has developed transparent and accessible brand valuation methodologies grounded in leading-edge marketing and investment practice. Brand Finance specializes in a range of services designed to maximize value in marketing and branding. These bespoke services include brand valuation, tracking, measuring, economics, strategy and communications.

Brand Finance works for a wide range of blue-chip clients, conducting national and international brand valuation and strategy assignments. Sectors covered include alcoholic beverages, automotive, banking, confectionery, information technology, insurance, food and telecommunications. For further information contact d.haigh@brandfinance.com

Innovation

IP is a major factor throughout the innovation process, not just at the end, argues Paul Leonard of the Intellectual Property Institute.

Contribution of IP to innovation

The DTI defines innovation as 'the commercial exploitation of good ideas'. Good ideas alone do not equal innovation. It is generally accepted that the UK is very good at generating good ideas, but less impressive when it comes to their commercial exploitation. One indicator is the fact that the UK hits way above its weight in citations in internationally recognized journals of physical science, biological science and medicine (third after the United States and former Soviet Union in total citations, and easily first if one corrects for population), but is well behind the United States in industrial productivity.

The IP system is not always a major factor in the generation of good ideas, particularly at the early, revolutionary stages of new technological development. Many of the very best ideas came about with no regard for patent protection, for example. It is certain, however, that the patent system plays a vital part in the commercial exploitation of those ideas, and that patent protection has been necessary to grow the often major companies and industries that emerged from them. It is also certain that research to provide new and improved products and processes costs money, and that the investment necessary to provide for this could often not be made without the IP system, for a broad range of industries. The financial contribution from commercial sources (often IP-generated) to academic endeavour within the university sector should also be recognized.

Successful branded goods companies, of which the UK has a significant number, could not justify their major investment in brand creation and support (often much larger than the R&D investment in creating the product) without IP protection for their trade marks. Much of the creative industry sector, from Andrew Lloyd Webber musicals to computer games software companies, would not exist without copyright protection.

Innovation depends upon a number of interrelated factors, and optimizing the climate for innovation is complex. The existence of an effective IP system is an essential, but not sole, requirement for successful innovation. It will not necessarily spur an increase in innovative activity in isolation from other, equally important, provisions.

I believe that a major gap in our knowledge is a very simple understanding of just how important IP is to the UK economy. If this were to be better understood, much else would flow from it. For example, several years ago the DTI published data showing that two-thirds of the market value of UK quoted companies was of 'knowledge-based companies'. Knowledge generates IP.

It is useful to examine what factors contribute to the establishment of an ideal climate in which to innovate, assessing how the IP system relates to these and how it can best promote them. If we look at 10 major factors, for example, IP rights are relevant in the following ways:

- the competitive cost of labour;
- the competitive cost of, and access to, capital (certainty/understanding of IP position);
- the competitive cost of raw materials;
- positive tax provisions (including IP licensing and technology transfer);
- a strong scientific/technical/creative base (with effective IP dissemination);
- minimal regulatory burden;
- a risk-embracing/entrepreneurial culture (which requires confidence in the legal position);
- a positive political climate that is technology-embracing;
- positive legal provisions (effective IP law and enforcement);
- strong corporate management and leadership (understanding the role of IP and strategy).

Innovation can loosely be described as a three-step process: research/invention, development, and commercial exploitation (including industry-wide diffusion). IP is often regarded as a factor that impacts mainly at the exploitation end of the innovation process. However, the above list demonstrates that IP is a major factor throughout the process, and perhaps most important in the middle phase, since this is where most of the financial risk occurs. In many industries there would be no investment if there were no patents to protect the invention and its subsequent commercialization, trade marks to protect the brand name, or copyright for the creative and computer sectors.

'Perfecting' the law so that it impacts positively across the innovation process is problematic for many reasons, but three major factors are:

- difficulty in achieving the right balance between the IP owner's rights and the benefits to society at large (through freedom of information, competition and so on);
- difficulty in defining what merits protection (especially with the advent of new technologies);
- difficulty in rationalizing global protection (in the face of legal, social and market differences).

Some examples of areas that would benefit from work to develop such knowledge and understanding are:

- IP and international trade and competition;
- IP valuation and benchmarking (including availability of data);
- access to litigation and enforcement (cost, speed and effectiveness);
- IP management and exploitation (benchmarking and best practice);
- the impact of IP on developing economies (with differing effects at different levels of economic development);
- IP regimes in the light of new technology;
- IP harmonization on a regional and global scale.

It is striking that business people, government officials and legislators in the United States have a much better knowledge of how the IP system works and its importance to the economy than do those in the UK. There is a good case for a long-term awareness programme in schools and universities to upgrade the basic knowledge of IP. A parallel might be the programme to improve entrepreneurialism through the schools programme initiated in the 1980s. The very positive impact of this is now becoming quite visible in the much more entrepreneurial graduates from our universities, but it has taken 15 years to give real results.

Concluding remarks

I firmly believe that the UK depends very heavily upon its ability to innovate to maintain economic success. The UK is well placed in this regard, since it has world-class strength in its creative, artistic, scientific and technological resources. The IP system plays a key role in turning these creative and inventive resources into commercial success and economic competitiveness. We believe, therefore, that the UK should strive to take a lead in developing our knowledge and understanding of IP law and its implementation in the global arena.

Dr Paul Leonard is Director of the Intellectual Property Institute, which aims to promote awareness and understanding of IP law (with particular emphasis on its economic and social impact), informing policy decisions and debate, through high-quality independent research. He is also chairman of the IP Awareness Group, an independent body dedicated to increasing awareness and understanding of IP. For further details contact 1st Floor, 36 Great Russell St., London WC1B 3QB; tel: 020 7436 3040; fax: 020 7323 5312; Web: www.ip-institute.org.uk

ERIC POTTER CLARKSON
PATENTS · TRADEMARKS · DESIGNS · COPYRIGHT

EPC

Areas of specialisation

Our firm has been specialising in intellectual property for over 100 years. We recognise that clients' needs require specialists either in technical subject matter or in different aspects of intellectual property. In order to address this need, we have over 30 patent attorneys dedicated to specialist areas of technology such as biotechnology, molecular biology, organic chemistry, medical chemistry, computing, electronics, telecommunications, medical engineering, materials science, computer software, mechanical engineering, pharmaceuticals, textiles, etc. Our dedicated trade mark attorneys handle trademark matters.

Supporting our team of professional attorneys, we have people qualified in other disciplines: information scientists, computer programmers, information technologists.

Main services include:

- Registration of patents, trademarks and registered designs in the UK, Europe and the rest of the world
- Validity and infringement opinions
- Searches for infringement clearance or validity
- Regular watches

Park View House
58 The Ropewalk
Nottingham NG1 5DD
United Kingdom

T. +44 (0) 115 955 2211
F. +44 (0) 115 955 2201
E. epc@eric-potter.com
W. www.eric-potter.com

BARKER BRETTELL

PATENTS TRADE MARKS COPYRIGHT DESIGNS

WHO WE ARE

Barker Brettell is one of the largest Intellectual Property firms in the UK with dedicated teams of Patent and Trademark specialists. We operate on a global level undertaking both UK originating work and International work generated through our contacts in 100+ countries.

The firm's headquarters is in Birmingham but we have presence across the UK in London, Cambridge and Southampton. We have over 40 Patent and Trademark Practitioners across our offices.

OUR COMMITMENT

- Provide a personal, highly efficient service that is second-to-none
- Get to know our clients and understand their needs to provide advice on all aspects of intellectual property protection
- Be proactive in the help we provide as well as offering a service that is excellent value for money

STRENGTH IN DEPTH

We have groups of experienced specialists who provide effective services across all technologies: Mechanical / Engineering; Electronics / Physics / Computer-related; Chemistry / Biotech; and Trademarks

OUR CORE SERVICES

- Drafting and filing patent and trademark applications
- IP Audits
- Patent and Trademark portfolio strategy / policy formulation
- Searches – novelty and clearance searches-

CONTINUOUS DEVELOPMENT

At Barker Brettell we consciously expand our portfolio of expertise in growth areas such as university clients; medical related inventions; computer and telecoms related inventions. Other growth areas include our trademark portfolio.

HOW TO CONTACT US

Further information can be obtained from John Lawrence, Practice Development Partner.

Telephone: (+44) 0121 456 0005;

E-mail: john.lawrence@barkerbrettell.co.uk

2
Building the portfolio

The intellectual property audit

Avoid costly blunders by running regular checks of what intellectual property (IP) you own, says Lawrence Smith-Higgins of the UK Patent Office.

Finding out what IP you own, and what you do not own, is one of the most reliable ways to reduce risk. A comprehensive audit of this kind may require a team of experts specializing in the various areas of IP, but a simple IP audit can be done by almost anyone if he or she knows what questions to ask.

First there is the 'internal' audit, used to identify IP for management purposes. The need here is to focus on the most important areas, and identify:

- Has your organization (or have you, as an individual) sufficient protection where it matters most?
- Has your organization IP that is redundant?
- If others use your organization's IP, what are the terms?
- Do contracts with employees or subcontractors adequately cover ownership?
- Has your organization proper procedures when disclosing confidential information?
- Who owns the IP?

Then there is the 'external' audit for identifying third-party IP:

- Does your organization use or intend to use third-party IP?
- Is the IP properly protected?
- Are proper licensing agreements in place?
- What precisely has been licensed?
- Is it being fully exploited?
- Is it possible to get similar IP free?
- Are regular searches conducted of IP databases?

These last two points can save plenty of money. If an organization is looking to buy in technology, it should not buy from the first company that has what it needs: some research should be done first. Check in patent databases to find a range of suppliers, and let them beat each other down on price. Indeed, some of the relevant patents might no longer be in force, so it might not even be necessary to buy a licence to copy the technology (although buying it in from the original inventors might still be cheaper).

A full audit will include all forms of IP, both 'hard' and 'soft'. The trick is to identify what IP exists and how to protect it effectively.

Checking what IP the organization owns

Businesses generally spend a lot of time and effort on names: the right name for the business or product could help it stand out from the crowd, while the wrong one could place it in a legal dispute. How important is the name of the company, and is it worth protecting with a registered trade mark (RTM)? If there are RTMs it is worth checking that procedures are in place to ensure that they are kept in force. Never overlook the obvious! One company that recently reviewed its RTM discovered that at the time of a management buy-out all assets had been transferred to the new management with the exception of the RTM. It did not own the company's main trade mark, and the registered owner was invoicing it for the renewal fees on the right to use it!

What about product names? A full IP review of the business might uncover other unexploited assets in the form of product names that have not been registered as trade marks. This could leave such products open to abuse by other companies. A more serious risk is the organization's inadvertent use of another company's trade mark, thus exposing it to possible legal action for infringement.

Has the organization any patented technology? If so it is important that protection is kept in force. Renewals have to be paid annually, and if this is not done the patent will lapse and become available for anyone to use. If the technology is not being used it could be worthwhile exploring the possibility of licensing it to others. (A few years ago a major manufacturer allowed a patent to lapse because the local managers believed the technology was obsolete, unaware that colleagues at another site were in negotiations to license the patent to a foreign firm!) Businesses must always seek to maximize the value extracted from IP, but if it is not being used and there is no likelihood of licensing it, why are they paying to keep it in force?

Does the organization license in any technology? If so, check the agreement and establish just what has been licensed. One company recently discovered that the licensing agreement it had entered into was on the basis of a certificate of grant which told it absolutely nothing about the extent of the patent! It had already spent a considerable amount of money in preparing the production process when this was realized.

Promoting any business is important. One company in particular found copyright ownership a very important issue when it carried out an audit. The company has a number of prestigious clients, and had engaged the services of a professional production company to produce a video of some of its work for these clients. Although this was an important asset for the company, it was one it did not own. It was a work protected by copyright, and the contractor – in this case the production company – had retained copyright ownership, and only licensed the company to make specific use of the video. Unauthorized use by the company of the video could land it in trouble.

A trade mark audit

This should include:

- ensuring that descriptive names are avoided for trade marks;
- checking that there are proper procedures for the registration and renewals processes;
- an assessment of future plans and product;
- discovery and recording of unregistered marks;
- review of any licensing agreements;
- regular review of the trade mark portfolio;
- regular trade mark searches to monitor legitimate usage;
- monitoring trade mark registers for similar marks registered by competitors.

A patent audit

This should include:

- checking that there are proper records of technical developments for assessment;
- checking that there are records of patents held and filed;

- checking on procedures for renewal;
- regular review of the patent portfolio, including licensing arrangements;
- a confidentiality review;
- a regular search of patents relevant to the business's activity.

The design audit

This should include:

- checking that records of designs are held and filed;
- checking on procedures for renewal;
- regular review of the design portfolio, including licensing arrangements;
- a regular search for designs relevant to the business's activity.

The copyright audit

This should include:

- ensuring that best practice is followed in affixing copyright notices;
- identifying and recording copyrights of commercial value;
- establishment of ownership;
- a review of licensing agreements.

These lists are in no way exhaustive, but serve to cover the kinds of issue that might be relevant to the business. In conducting and establishing an audit process it is important to identify what is to be accomplished and to make sure that this is achieved. It is also important to record the entire process. In all instances someone should be assigned responsibility for these issues in his or her job description.

The record of any audit should include the objective, the plan and how it was executed. It should describe and evaluate the intellectual property issues, and propose recommendations for improvements, with a timescale for review. It goes without saying that the audit should be treated as commercially sensitive.

Stay regular

Focusing on issues such as these is the first stage in working out the IP strategy that fits the business best. A regular review of IP is far more desirable, and a lot easier, than putting it off until something happens that forces the organization to look at it. If IP is left unprotected, it could be lost to those that are better placed to commercialize it, leaving its originator without any financial gain. A simple audit is a good place to start. Recognizing what IP is present and taking adequate steps to protect it should enable the organization to take advantage of the IP system and profit from creativity. Good, regular management of IP is even better.

Lawrence Smith-Higgins joined the Patent Office in 1989, and worked in several different departments before moving to marketing in 2000. He is engaged in the publicizing and marketing of the Patent Office and its services, mainly through seminars and workshops for business advisors and academics, and writing articles for the national and specialist press. His work involves partnerships with organizations such as Business Link (in England), Scottish Enterprise, Invest NI, and Business Eye (in Wales).

Lawrence also works with the Inland Revenue and HM Customs & Excise to provide growing businesses with basic guidance about IP. The guidance comes in the form of seminars at Business Advice Open Days which are held throughout the UK and attended by Patent Office staff.

For more information about any aspect of IP, visit www.patent.gov.uk or call 08459 500 505.

HEPWORTH LAWRENCE BRYER & BIZLEY
PATENT & TRADEMARK ATTORNEYS

www.ipforbusiness.com

You can use the link above but if you would like a free
IP For Business CD please telephone 01992 561756
or email: special@hlbb.com

Searching IP databases

IP databases are bursting with expertise, says Dr Jeremy Philpott of the Patent Office. So check them first, before committing funds to R&D or a new brand.

During the Second World War, British bomb disposal teams were desperate to find safe ways to defuse unexploded bombs (UXBs). Such bombs caused far more disruption to the war effort than their brothers that went 'bang' in the night – streets, stations and factories could remain closed for many days if an unexploded bomb was found. To extract a working bomb fuse, upon which studies could be made, was the Holy Grail of UXB teams. But working fuses did their job and left nothing to examine, whereas the fuses which could be recovered were duds, and hence hardly appropriate for unlocking the secrets of the Luftwaffe's ordnance. Then in 1942, Ministry of Defence scientists found the patent for Ruhlemann's electric bomb fuse, as used during the Blitz, and within two weeks of studying the full, clear and complete technical description therein they were able to issue a bulletin to all the UXB teams explaining how to safely defuse such weapons. The tragedy is that the patent had been published and lain in the Patent Library since 1931. How many died trying to defuse those bombs when the solution was at hand all along?

Fear of unwitting infringement is what tends to drive people to check the registers for designs and trade marks. Given that the registers are freely accessible over the Internet, there can be no excuse for inadvertently branding a new business with a word or logo that is already registered to someone else. Getting a new company name registered at Companies House, and a domain name registered with Nominet or the Internet Corporation for Assigned Names and Numbers (ICANN), will be a waste of time if an injunction is served by the owner of a registered trade mark that is the same as the new business name. So before an individual or organization settles on a name for a new business, product or service, it should at least spend a few minutes checking the trade marks register. And if it wants to stop others jumping on the reputation it hopes to acquire under a name, it should seek appropriate registration for that name.

Existing brand owners also want to check that competitors are not attempting to register trade marks that are too similar to their own. This is why trade marks are published ('advertised') three months prior to registration: to allow others to check that marks that might be confusingly similar to their own, and that might threaten to dilute their brand, are not getting onto the register.

It is perfectly possible for a firm to infringe another's patent without ever owning one of its own. However, the reasons for checking patent databases extend far beyond the simple fear of infringement. They go to the core purpose for having a patent system in the first place. The State grants limited exclusive rights to those creating new technologies in exchange for clear and complete disclosure of those technologies. This encourages innovation by rewarding disclosure rather than secrecy. The disclosure is there to benefit the public at large, and competitors' R&D teams specifically.

Patent databases are bursting with technical expertise. Over 45 million patents from around the world can be accessed over the Internet through a variety of databases. Why would anyone want to spend money on R&D to develop a solution to a problem that has already been solved and disclosed in a patent? Nevertheless, the EU Commission estimates that €20 billion is wasted every year in Europe on R&D for technologies already disclosed in patents.

Commercial providers of patent information often quote an estimate that 80 per cent of all technical disclosures appearing in patents do not appear anywhere else. While this might not be possible to verify, many patent examiners would concur, particularly based on their experience of dealing with patent applications coming from academics. It is commonplace to see academic papers that conclude with a dozen or more references to other relevant academic papers. Rarely do such papers reference patents, yet a patent search on the subject often turns up numerous relevant patents. Patents reference academic papers more frequently than *vice versa*. The bottom line is that any researcher who only consults trade journals and academic papers to determine the 'state of the art' is missing the vast majority of what is being said about new developments: he or she needs to also be looking at patent publications.

A manufacturing company once struggled to develop a new paint. It had been successful at the pilot scale in the laboratory, but in bulk manufacturing it hit unforeseen and seemingly insurmountable problems. It went to a commercial patent search service, and paid for a trawl of all the relevant literature to find any patent for a similar paint that might describe a solution to its problem. Two days later the results were ready, and the manufacturer was astonished to find that an old patent described precisely the paint formulation it was trying to make, for the same intended application. It described the problem the company had hit, explained what caused it, and prescribed a remedy. The patent was 30 years old, and as such was long since lapsed and free for anyone to copy. Although delighted to discover the solution to all its problems, the manufacturer was chagrined to learn that it had itself been the applicant on the old patent! This shows that it should have been looking back through its own R&D records. The message for everyone else is that looking in patent databases is like having a free rummage through all your competitors' R&D records.

Patent databases are a truly awesome source of competitive intelligence. Applications for patents are usually published 18 months after their first filing date (or sooner), often while a product is still being refined in the laboratory, and long before any rights are granted. This gives firms an early warning as to what their competitors' latest products are likely to be. Pharmaceutical products are the ones that take the longest to get to market, so the patents behind them are well understood by the industry years before a pill is sold. Conversely, the short product lifetimes in the software and telecoms sector tend to mean that the published patents lag somewhat behind the market place, but they are still a useful source of technical data.

Patents are classified according to technology type, and the databases can be searched using those classifications. So it is possible to isolate, for example, the 10,000 documents classified in a specific area of technology, and run a statistical analysis for the frequency of the applicants' names. Competitors that are well known might appear near the top of the list, each owning several dozen patents. But some of the names will be unfamiliar: find out who they are! Are they rivals, or potential allies? Do they have technology that the organization might want to license, or does it have something to license to them? Is it possible to spot a gap in another organization's technology portfolio, or perhaps some complementary product it might need? If so – invent it, patent it and license it to that organization in exchange for whatever your organization wants from it!

Whose technology is 'leading edge'? An answer can be found by performing an analysis on relevant patents, sorted by date. It might turn up dozens and dozens of patents owned by a conventional competitor, that are all more than five years old, while the organization has no recent applications for new developments, showing that it is no longer inventing in the sector, and its technology is becoming obsolete. Conversely, a firm whose products you have never seen might have been filing patents in a coveted market at the rate of one per month for the last two years. Read what they are doing, and start running to catch up!

Does the organization need to poach the best R&D engineer in its sector? Do a statistical analysis for the inventors' names given on relevant patents. An inventor's employer is likely to be the patent applicant, and this tells rivals from where to head-hunt him or her.

Do not be disheartened if the organization's next great product happens to be the subject of a published patent application. This does not automatically mean that it risks infringing another organization's patent. Foreign inventions may be copied in the UK provided there is no equivalent UK patent, and provided the products are not imported into the country of registration. It is also worth remembering that 50 per cent of the patent applications published by the Patent Office are never granted. Of those that are granted, all must be renewed annually to be kept in force, and only 5 per cent are so renewed up to the 20 year maximum lifetime. This means that the vast majority of patents appearing in the databases are free to be read and copied if: they were never granted; or were not kept in force; or do not relate to a territory where the organization plans to make, use, import or sell its product. However, while you, or your own organization, are free to copy such technologies, so is everyone else. Now that those inventions have been published, no one can later obtain a valid patent to exclude others from using them.

All of this analysis is perfectly legal, and has nothing to do with spending money on a patent portfolio. The savings for R&D and the opportunities to identify rivals and allies at an early stage are just too great to be ignored.

For more information about any aspect of IP visit www.patent.gov.uk or call 08459 500 505.

Application tactics

Where and when you apply for IP can have far-reaching implications, says John Gray at Fitzpatricks.

Legal protection for ideas (often called 'intellectual property' or 'IP') is available in various forms. Even if it is known in general terms what type of protection is needed, it can make a big difference how you go about it in terms of timing, selection of countries and so on. This chapter aims to provide a rough guide to the factors that will influence the tactics.

Perfect timing

Most countries use the date of filing as a simple and fair way to decide which has priority between two competing applications, so it is important to file the application at the Patent Office before another person (or organization) files for the same thing or something similar. Do not leave it too late. Especially for *patents* and *designs*, the chances of protection can be spoilt if the invention is disclosed before a complete patent application is filed. It is important to ensure that no-one in the organization releases details of the invention or puts it on sale before protection is in place.

It is not possible to tell straight away whether someone else has filed for the same idea, but if it is suspected that others are working on the same problem, it would be wise to file sooner rather than later. Total secrecy is not always an option. It might be necessary for the inventor to tell someone about it, for example to get engineering advice or prototypes made, or to raise funds for development. A formal confidentiality agreement (also called a non-disclosure agreement or NDA) might provide enough protection for these limited disclosures, but if the project has reached a stage where it requires some non-confidential disclosure in order to proceed, it is time to file the patent application.

For *trade marks*, it is not quite so important to file the application before using the mark, but the organization runs the risk that others will file first if it does not. On the other hand, some marks (such as common surnames) only become distinctive enough to be registered after a few years' use. For such marks, it is possible to use the '™' marking in the meantime (the '®' symbol must only be used on registered marks). It is also possible to file an application to register the mark combined with some other distinctive elements for the time being.

In the UK and EU, it is even possible to file for a *design registration* up to a year after the design has been published, so market testing is possible. Some countries (notably the United States) also allow a similar 'grace period' for patents.

Or should we wait?

Assuming there is no pressing reason that the patent application must be filed immediately, it can be a difficult judgement when is the best time to file it. Although all will be lost if the organization is not the first to file an application for the same invention, there are other considerations that might well justify delaying until the time is right:

- The invention might not be sufficiently complete. An 'enabling disclosure' is a fundamental legal requirement for a patent to be valid.
- Filing a patent application starts a number of legal 'clocks' ticking, so that further action and expense will follow within fixed time limits. Therefore filing sooner brings forward the costs of drafting, foreign filing, examination and renewal fees. For many individual inventors and SMEs, applications simply have to be abandoned because capital or income to fund the next stage is not in place in time.
- The ideas will be published sooner, perhaps before they are fully developed. Others with greater resources might then be able to steal a march, or develop ways to work around the patent.
- The patent will expire sooner. For many developments, 20 years turns out to be not as long as it looked at the outset!

It is possible to hedge one's bet to some extent by filing an application to establish a place in the queue, so to speak, while the innovation is being developed further or the commercial prospects are investigated. Sometimes it is appropriate to expand and re-file the patent application one or more times during the course of the first year after filing, to get the earliest possible 'priority date' for each aspect of the development. So long as the invention remains secret, it is possible to withdraw the application and re-file it later to restart the clock. Once the invention is publicly disclosed, however, there is no going back.

World domination

The UK is a relatively small market and the investment in product development, marketing, patenting and other IP protection is rarely justified for the UK market alone. There is no single 'worldwide patent', and a British patent has no force in other countries. If the organization wants any control of activities in Germany or Taiwan, for example, it will therefore want to protect the mark, invention or design by registrations in those countries.

Let's file everywhere then!

Unfortunately, seeking protection abroad can be costly, especially for patents. Few small businesses can afford to protect inventions or marks straight away in dozens of countries, and large businesses also need to control their costs by selecting countries carefully. Bear in mind also that further costs will arise for examination and grant procedures, so it is wise not to spend the whole IP budget by filing in too many countries.

Happily, several international agreements and procedures are in place that allow patentees to defer the costs of protection in individual countries, but those costs cannot be put off indefinitely.

Deciding where to file

It is sometimes useful to establish certain preferred filing patterns: for example a long list of countries for major developments and a shorter list for minor improvements, or different lists for 'professional' and 'consumer' product ranges. The organization might target:

- key markets;
- competitors' key markets;
- its manufacturing base;
- its competitors' manufacturing bases;
- important trade routes (such as Hong Kong).

To cover all of the above provides a 'belt and braces'. Having protection where competitors manufacture could allow the organization to take action against infringers at source, more cheaply than pursuing them in every market. Even if it does not intend to market its products in a far-off land, having a patent there can be a useful bargaining counter against a competitor based there, who has a patent in the organization's key market for something the organization would like to use.

Particularly for inventions where the cost of setting up manufacture is only justified if large markets can be addressed, it might be sufficient to protect a few major markets, in order to keep out competitors. For products or services that can be manufactured easily anywhere, however only local protection will protect local markets.

In many cases, brands or technologies are developed for franchising, selling on, or licensing to larger players, as a way of sharing the risk and capital requirements of the 'global market place'. If this is the plan (and if the organization is not already a global player it is usually the only realistic plan), then it goes without saying that there should be protection in every territory where the organization wishes to sign up such partners.

Since trade marks are all about protecting a distinct identity in the market place, important trade marks should be registered in all the organization's markets. It might also be desirable to protect them in major future markets when launching at home. Some trade mark originators have found that their mark is literally not their own when they come to enter a foreign market, because a local trader has seen it and registered it for itself first.

As well as being limited to certain territory, trade mark registrations are also limited to particular ranges of goods and/or services. Because the cost to register a mark depends partly on how many 'classes' of goods and services are to be covered, and because of the need to avoid clashes with other people's use of similar marks for different types of goods and services, not all goods and services might be registered from the outset. As time goes by, however, it is important to review coverage as the organization's reputation and business grows. A little foresight in choosing and protecting their brands makes this whole process go a lot more smoothly for some companies than others!

Do your homework

As the saying goes, 'great minds think alike'. With over 45 million patent documents indexed and searchable free on the Web, there is even less excuse for 'reinventing the wheel' than there ever was before. There is also a risk of investing in a new idea or brand that turns out to be blocked by other people's patents or trade mark registrations. Therefore it is advisable to perform novelty searches and/or infringement clearance searches before filing. The search results might show that some negotiation with others is needed, to gain the freedom that is needed to exploit ideas or brands. This negotiation will be easier if the organization has not committed millions in manufacturing, printing and television advertising before the problem comes to light!

Ask the experts

Very few business people have the time to master all these considerations for themselves, and mistakes can turn out very costly, or even irreparable. Experienced help can be found if you know where to look. The key is for organizations to understand their markets and competitors, and know how they want their business to develop into the future. Once they have that, professional advisers such as Chartered Patent Attorneys and Trade Mark Attorneys can help guide them to a balanced and cost-effective programme of registration. These experts should be consulted at the start of any new product development. Even if you may feel there will be little for them to do at that stage, a little guidance could avoid some costly mistake.

John J Gray is a Senior Patent Attorney with Fitzpatricks, Chartered Patent Attorneys and Trade Mark Attorneys. John has over 17 years' experience in obtaining and advising on patents, particularly in electronic and computer software technologies, but also in subsea construction and miscellaneous other fields. He worked in a multinational industrial patent department before entering practice. Fitzpatricks is based in Glasgow and serves clients not only from Scotland but across the UK and also world-wide, to obtain and advise on the full range of intellectual property rights, including patents, trade marks, registered designs and copyright. Inventions in a wide range of technologies are handled by technically qualified specialists. The expertise and resources of Fitzpatricks' own Patent and Trade Mark Attorneys is supplemented by a world-wide network of associates experienced in local law and practice. Fitzpatricks today continues a business founded in 1887 by Hugh Donald Fitzpatrick. 'Fitzpatricks' is (of course) a registered trade mark.

Strategic patenting

Patents are not simply expensive pieces of paper. If used strategically, they are an effective commercial weapon and a significant business asset, advises Drew Lamb of Urquhart-Dykes & Lord, LLP.

Strategic patenting is concerned with developing and utilizing a patent portfolio to assist in achieving set business aims. While patents might primarily be thought of as an aspect of high-tech companies, in reality patents and patent strategies can be used in a wide range of businesses. Just as there are a variety of businesses and business models, so there are a variety of patent strategies.

What patents can be used for

A patent's most basic use is to protect a product, or method of making a product, from being copied. However, patents have much wider uses. If publicized, a comprehensive patent portfolio in a particular technical field can deter a competitor from even entering that field, simply for fear of infringement. At the very least, the patent holder will put a competitor to the time and expense of designing around its patents, which will hopefully result in a less commercial product.

Patents can also reserve for the patent holder an area of technology for future use and exploitation. In view of the requirement that a patentable invention must be new, the filing of what might be a speculative patent application it can prevent others from later trying to patent the same invention, which could restrict their use and further development of the technology.

A patent can be selectively licensed, allowing others to produce the product or use the method in return for a royalty or other benefit. As a result, licensed patents can directly generate a revenue stream. Patents can also be used to gain access to related areas of technology covered by the patent, which the patent holder does not have the resources to exploit, or to produce new products through cross-licensing and exchanges with other patent holders.

A patent is a type of property with a value, just like any other business asset such as a building or machine. Indeed for a number of companies, patents form a key part of the value of the business. As with other assets, patents can attract investors, they can be sold and traded, and they can be borrowed against.

A comprehensive patent portfolio demonstrates a level of innovation and original thinking within a company, which is attractive to would-be investors, collaborators and customers, and threatening to competitors.

As a marketing tool patents can highlight the innovative nature of a company (as indicated by Hewlett Packard's 'HP Invent' slogan), or to attach a level of exclusivity or cachet to a product, for example the Dyson vacuum cleaner.

An impenetrable thicket

When considering patents strategically, the business must drive the strategy, rather than the quantum of technological merit involved. It is often possible, and profitable, to obtain a patent for a modest technological improvement, and so patent protection should not be reserved only for giant leaps forward. The basic consideration is how the patent will be used to achieve a business end, and to assist in building a coherent and business-directed portfolio of patents.

For example, if the aim is simply to protect a new invention comprehensively, it is much better to have a number of patents, each covering different aspects of the invention, rather than a single patent. A single patent is more straightforward for a competitor to design around or invalidate. In contrast, a thicket of related patents often appears far more impenetrable.

Alternative uses

It is also important to patent alternatives to the main commercial embodiments of the invention. Otherwise, the organization leaves the door open to its competitors to use and patent these alternatives themselves. Protecting alternatives in this way also sets the innovation as far apart from competitor products as possible, and allows for future developments and changes. In addition, such a strategy can mask the most commercial version of a product, or best methodology, so providing a key advantage.

Improvements

Similarly, it is essential to patent any improvements to the basic invention, in order not only to extend the life of patent protection (a patent lasts a maximum of 20 years) but also to maintain protection as technology and the market develops.

Conversely, if the organization operates in an area of technology in which a competitor holds only a few key patents, by filing a number of patents to possible improvements to the basic concept it can restrict and curtail the competitor's future development of the field. The 'improvement' patents can then be used as leverage to negotiate a licence for the key patent. In this way the organization might gain access to a field that is closed to the market in general, and benefit from the competitor's patents.

Searches

By actively feeding back the results of searches carried out as part of the patenting process to the development team, details of existing patents and the technical teaching can be usefully identified and utilized. It is estimated that one-third of all money spent on R&D is spent reinventing technology already in the public domain. Significant money can therefore be saved by using the results of patent searches. Details of earlier patents which may present infringement problems can also be identified through the patent search process.

Timing

The timing of patent filings is also important. For an area of established technology, patents for improvements can be staggered over time to maintain a strong portfolio, and present an impression that expertise in that field is keeping pace with developments. Alternatively, for a ground-breaking development, it can be beneficial to file the maximum number of patents over a relatively short time period, to present competitors with an impressive armoury. Similarly when building a company, either initially or for disposal, a significant and young patent portfolio can enhance the business assets.

Ambush and disguise

Ownership of the patent rights is a further consideration of any strategy. Patents may be obtained in the name of an apparently unrelated company in order to disguise an interest while the patent portfolio is being established.

This may be used to ambush a competitor that has patent watches only in relation to particular company names. In addition, as patents are an asset that can give rise to licence revenue, a strategy associating ownership of development work with a particular company within a group can be devised to enhance inter-company financial arrangements. Some multinationals use holding companies to own and license their collective patent portfolio.

Collaboration

If a business is involved in any form of collaborative work, patents should be sought for all new and commercially significant aspects, to clearly capture, identify, and stake ownership for any innovation developed under the joint programme. In this way, the resulting patent portfolio demarcates and defines the results of the collaboration. This not only reflects the value of the partnership, but can also avoid future conflict and argument between the parties.

Who are you going to sue?

A final consideration in any strategy is to consider who, ultimately, would be sued under any patent. This might be a competing manufacturer, a customer, supplier or defaulting licensee. This in turn will determine the scope of patent protection sought, and the countries covered. For example, the fact the main customers for a product are based in one country might suggest that patent protection be filed for in that country. However, if a supplier would never sue a customer or potential customer, the patent holder needs to ensure that protection is also obtained where other competing suppliers are based.

How patent strategies should be developed

The development of a successful patent strategy requires a close and continual liaison between the innovators, patent attorneys, marketeers and business management. By working closely together, patents can be developed and effectively utilized as a key additional business tool and asset to further business goals.

For further information contact Drew Lamb at Urquhart-Dykes & Lord, LLP New Priestgate House, 57 Priestgate, Peterborough, PE1 1JX; tel: +44 1733 340011; fax: +44 1733 566387; e-mail: peterborough@udl.co.uk

Outward licensing

Licensing IP can be a highly effective way of expanding internationally, argues Guy Reeves, Chairman of the Institute of International Licensing Practitioners.

The managing director of Goodwidgets Ltd has reason to be proud of his company. The last three years' R&D programme is now beginning to pay off as sales of the latest new products exceed forecasts. And the recently commissioned technology audit has identified several potentially rewarding opportunities from the company's intellectual property (IP) portfolio ripe for exploitation. Whilst Goodwidgets has a well-established sales and marketing capability in the UK where it is based, commercializing its IP assets in those overseas markets that have been identified as having promise requires careful thought. The MD now needs to decide the best strategy for implementing the business development programme. He considers the following options:

- Launch a major export sales drive – fine for finished patented products, but otherwise irrelevant.
- Establish exclusive distributorship agreements. Such arrangements might also include an option whereby the distributors become licensees, manufacturing locally, if sales develop well. Again, fine for physical products but not for technologies, processes or other forms of IP rights.
- Set up local subsidiaries overseas with sound sales and marketing capabilities – a risky option, heavily demanding of management resources and capital investment.
- Explore joint venture agreements.

- Acquire companies that are able to exploit the IP in the markets offering potential.
- Sell the IP rights outright for as high a price as possible.
- License out the IP.

As an international marketing and business development tool the advantages and flexibility of outward licensing can be considerable:

- By making use of established local production, marketing and sales facilities, a licensor avoids the need for and associated risks of setting up complete manufacturing and marketing facilities from first principles.
- Costly investment in tooling and machinery is obviated.
- No export financing is required, nor are there problems of supply or labour to face.
- Promotional and selling costs become the licensee's responsibility.
- By virtue of the nature of a licence agreement, a licensee is likely to have a far greater commitment to the IP or new product than an agent or distributor.

It is important to understand that there is no such thing as a standard licence agreement: each is individually negotiated according to the circumstances of the desired commercial arrangement. There are, however, certain fundamental components that should be included in most licence agreements:

1. A description of the rights being granted and their fields of use – or permitted application. A licence agreement gives the licensee the right(s) to make and/or use and/or sell the IP, which may be protected by one or more of the conventional protective mechanisms (patent, registered design, copyright or design right). Moreover, the IP may take the form of – or involve – unprotected know-how or trade secrets, knowledge that is believed to be outside the common domain and that may outlast the life of the patent.
2. The type of licence being granted, of which there are essentially three types:
   - exclusive licence – where the rights are granted, as the term implies, exclusively to the licensee;
   - sole licence – where the rights are granted to a sole licensee while at the same time retained by the owner;
   - non-exclusive licence – where the rights are granted to two or more licensees.
   Understandably, the terms of each type tend to reflect the degree of monopoly being granted.

3. The geographic franchise for which the rights are being granted – since formal protection for IP is arranged on a territorial basis.
4. The period for which the licence is to apply.
5. Payment terms. The main form of payment for a licence is usually royalties – a pre-agreed amount paid for each product sold or, in the case of a process, usage made of the IP. It is important that the basis of calculation for royalties is precise and unambiguous.

    There are, however, forms of payment in addition to royalties that may be included in a licence agreement:

    - A down payment – a lump sum, usually paid on the signing of the licence agreement, although staged payments may be appropriate. It is normally negotiated in recognition of the scope of the commercial opportunity being assigned and the R&D investment that the licensee has been spared. A down payment is distinct from and wholly unconnected to whatever royalty rate payment formula may be agreed. But perhaps the most important purpose of a down payment is to encourage the licensee company to work the licence: it is more likely to do this if it has had to part with a lump sum of money.
    - A pre-payment, as the term implies, is an advance payment of royalties: a pre-agreed sum, paid on the signing of the agreement, against which royalties on sales are retroactively set, as and when they fall due. A pre-payment is often agreed where a down payment is either inappropriate or cannot be negotiated.
    - Fees for consultancy services.
6. Although not essential, it is usual for a licence between willing parties to include minimum annual performance criteria. These may take the form of minimum annual royalties, and constitute further inducement to the licensee actively to work the licence, while providing a measure of security to the licensor.
7. Provision for termination. The agreement should clearly set out the grounds on which termination by either party may be initiated. Either party may give an agreed period of notice to the other during the term of the agreement, or it may be that a breach of contract or failure by either party to perform pre-agreed obligations constitutes grounds for termination.

In searching for suitable prospective licensees there are certain key factors to be considered:

■ Size of company. The largest companies in the market place do not always make the best licensee partners. They may not need – or be as motivated – to make such a success of a new product as companies in the second division which have a greater incentive to grow and become leaders in their field.

- Sales and marketing capability. Whilst a prospect may have the necessary production facilities, it is crucial that it is able to demonstrate strong marketing, distribution and selling resources. Royalties, after all, are normally paid on sales, not on manufacture.
- Reason for interest. Every prospective licensee will have a reason for being attracted to new IP, and it is important to establish as early as possible what that reason is. Some prospects may feign genuine interest while simply wishing to gain intelligence about new developments affecting their market; or – more insidiously – they may want to block from the market new technology that could threaten their own position. Others may have genuine commercial reasons for wanting a licence – facilitating entry to a new product sector, a new geographic market or to a hitherto untapped distribution channel, perhaps. The reasons can vary widely, but only when it has been discovered why a prospect wants a licence is it possible to assess that prospect's potential compatibility as a partner in terms of what it needs from and will contribute to the licence.
- Enthusiasm – an infectious, but vitally important quality. If a prospect is not highly motivated at the start of discussions, it is unlikely to be the right partner to commercialize the IP rights.

At the end of the day a licence agreement binds two parties together in a commercial partnership. Having agreed terms, neither party should feel it has won more than it deserved; nor should either party feel it has lost out. There should be no post-agreement resentment. The most successful licences are when both parties privately acknowledge that the terms are fair, and are enthusiastic about the challenge of building a successful, long-term business founded on new, exciting technology and other IP rights.

Guy Reeves is Chairman and Fellow of the Institute of International Licensing Practitioners. The Institute of International Licensing Practitioners was founded in England in 1969 to set, promote and maintain high standards of professional practice among those engaged in licensing intellectual property rights, technology transfer and commercializing invention. It was the first organization of its kind in the English-speaking world, and has members world-wide. Entry to membership is strictly by election and is subject to appropriate qualifications and experience. Through its strict Code of Professional Conduct, by which all members have agreed to be bound, the Institute is the only professional body in the English-speaking world that regulates the activities of licensing professionals.

For further information contact the Institute of International Licensing Practitioners, Oxford Centre for Innovation, Mill Street, Oxford, OX2 0JX, England, tel: +44(0)1865 812060; fax: +44(0)1865 793165; e-mail: enquiries@iilp.net; Web site: www.iilp.net

Risk?

The hidden risks of intellectual property (IP) can have enormous commercial impact for both investors and companies alike.

Gill Jennings & Every has built an international reputation proactively managing these IP risks through innovative solutions that add value.

We advise on the development of IP strategies as an integral part of business planning, fund raising and investment. Contact us for an initial review.

Can you afford to wait until the hidden risks emerge?

Gill Jennings & Every

European Patent Attorneys
European Trade Mark Attorneys

Licensing in

Licensed-in technology, designs or brands can all be remarkably cheap and effective drivers of business growth, although it is a strategy often neglected by British companies, says John D Emanuel of Pax Technology Transfer.

Introduction

Curiously, most authoritative works on licensing take a highly skewed view of the subject, looking at it almost exclusively from the potential licensor's licensing-out point of view: How does it find licensees? How does it maximize royalties? How does it minimize tax? And so on. But for commercial companies, finding and licensing in patented technology and other intellectual property – becoming a licensee – can be even more important. ***Licensed-in technology, designs or coveted brands can all be remarkably cheap and effective drivers of business growth***. It is a strategy often neglected by British companies.

At the core of most outstanding businesses' success are intellectual property rights (IPR), rights that hold the competition at arm's length – know-how and trade secrets, patents, copyright, brands and trade marks. Indeed, outstandingly successful businesses take every opportunity to differentiate themselves from the general competition by building their IPR assets. Some of these rights will be generated internally, but it is now recognized that the mould-breaking transforming innovations are more than likely to come from outside.

A drug discovery from a university, a novel process, an iconic design or a trusted or valued logo acquired under licence: all can transform a business.

Black & Decker had the vision to license in the Workmate (a device that combines a vice and a sawhorse). Reckitt & Coleman had the vision to license in a remedy it branded Gaviscon (now sold by GlaxoSmithKline). A garment branded under licence 'Manchester United' can be worth double or more than double the unbranded equivalent.

Patented improvements help extend the period of protection from direct competition. For example, pharmaceutical companies patent innovative delivery technologies for a successful drug, reducing the effect of competition from generic versions.

A company that wants to acquire innovative IPR – a proactive potential licensee – can offer a licensor a number of very attractive characteristics. First, a company actively searching and willing and resolved to take up good opportunities is highly encouraging to a potential licensor. Second, the potential licensee might be well established, with a good reputation, and have easy access to and a good understanding of the market. It might also have the resources that the licensor lacks to scale up a project.

A well-established licensee is therefore in a particularly strong position to secure a deal on terms favourable to itself. It is usually a licensees' market out there!

'Narrow' searches

If the need for highly specific IPR has been well defined, for example to avoid infringing a patent or to secure rights to make a specific product enhancement, the need can be analysed and the potential licensor or licensors pinpointed. This involves entering keywords into the right search engine on the World Wide Web, into suitable directories – patent and other databases – and bingo, out pops a list of possibilities. This type of search can be called a 'narrow' search.

Is the organization seeking better treatments for burns patients? There are several top quality research groups that can offer the very latest technology. Does it need optical photoconductive drum technology? There are companies out there who would offer a licence or even a joint venture. Does it want to improve its cold forging operation for making automotive parts? There are companies in Germany, Japan and the United States who would be very happy to talk to it. Would it like to embellish a product or service with Rupert Bear's or David Beckham's image? Just ask!

This search approach works well for licensors that *an organization knows it needs*. Narrow searches are easy to carry out and effective in identifying improvements to existing products and services. But 'narrow' searches, effective as they can be, identify only those licensing opportunities that are already known to the potential licensee.

As a creative tool for a more ambitious business growth strategy 'narrow' searches are too limited.

'Wide', creative searches

There exists an almost unlimited range of IPR around the world that, in theory at least, could be made available to a company. Within this unlimited range, certain licensing opportunities will be particularly relevant and attractive to any specific company, given its skills, its marketing capability, its culture and its financial resources. Many of these licensing opportunities might be 'dormant', not even having been formulated in the mind of the potential licensor! When a potential licensee 'knocks on the door' and expresses interest in some IPR, it is often only then that the potential licensor awakens to the opportunity.

Bigger opportunities in business tend to arise from tricks of fate as much as from logical linear thought and action. A chance meeting, an article in a newspaper, an invention, a technology from a different market sector, a drastic cost reduction, a 'Eureka!' moment, are often the initiators of major profitable new activities. What took Nokia, an apparently stolid and not very profitable Finnish paper company, into mobile phones? What took Black & Decker, a power tool manufacturer, into sawhorses and vices? Who planned to make and sell penicillin? What happened when the cost of micro-processors tumbled?

Somewhere out there in the world, there are licensing and other opportunities relevant to each company. A Japanese group wants to license its technology to a UK company to serve the European market. A high-tech company in California wants an industrial partner for Europe. A research organization has made a surprise breakthrough. How does a company identify such opportunities relevant to itself? How can it find potential licensors that can offer the technology to take the company forward into the next century? How can it find and select the licensor(s), the technologies and other IPR that will be crucial to it – *even those it does not know it needs?*

Powerful methodologies have been developed over the last 20 years to carry out this type of business opportunity search – effectively a global brainstorm focused on the aspirations of a particular company. Search services are offered by certain technology transfer companies specializing in this type of work and by some of the larger management consulting companies. With their deep experience and wide range of contacts around the world, these specialists can be far more efficient 'wide' searchers than any company operating in a limited group of market sectors.

A useful tool for a 'wide' search technique is a written profile of the company, which outlines its areas of interest and its aspirations. Outside help is often needed to help an organization articulate its aspirations into a form that others can understand and will act upon.

The profile is distributed as widely as possible to intermediaries – technology transfer specialists, business consultants, venture capitalists, scientific attachés, trade associations, selected professors, university licensing offices, licensing offices of big organizations – for their ideas and the breadth of their contacts, and is also posted on specialist technology databases on the Web. Intermediaries will identify opportunities not only in the sector defined but also in adjacent or complementary sectors and markets that might be highly pertinent. The profile should also go out to 'friends and family' – the company's professional advisers, selected suppliers and customers, its consultants and its employees.

The selection process

The combination of 'narrow and 'wide' searches will generate many opportunities for the company, some good, some bad, some obvious and some less obvious. The sheer volume of opportunities generated by a wide search can be challenging. It is important therefore to create and manage an effective selection process so that poor opportunities are discarded as early as possible to avoid management overload, and excellent opportunities are identified, characterized and pursued.

Typically a company might have to look at a hundred or more apparent opportunities for each one it takes up. This statistic is not as daunting as it seems at first sight. Of the opportunities some 50 per cent can be discarded after cursory examination and a further 40 per cent after minor consideration. With a little luck, some jewels will be among the rest.

Finding, selecting, negotiating and closing a deal can take time. Typically, from the initiation of the search to the time that the new product or service is found and secured will take 3–18 months.

Choice

It is not that a company merely needs a licensing or other business development opportunity; it needs to expose itself to a choice of opportunities from the best available. The 'wide' and 'narrow' search approach is a strategic technique to identify opportunities from which can be selected the best and most appropriate for a given company at a given stage in its history and development.

A metaphor for the process is the Wimbledon tennis championship. The greatest excitement is in the quarter-finals, the semi-finals and the finals. To have some outstanding players or outstanding projects to compete in the final, it is necessary to start with promising players and projects from all around the world.

The business of licensing

Because licence agreements are somewhat complex and extend over many years, and because there is a substantial body of law that affects licensing, much of it changing progressively, licensing literature tends to emphasize the legal aspects of licensing. But licensing is a business activity. A company can license-in to enhance its production capabilities and range of product offerings. It can also license-out to enhance its penetration into additional industrial sectors and geographical markets. Both these activities can be used to create powerful business development and business expansion strategies.

The challenges are:

■ to find, select and introduce new products, enhancements, technologies, designs and brands into the current business (licensing in)
■ to use IPR to ensure other companies penetrate and exploit markets outside the company's reach (licensing out).

Companies should aim to become both serial licensees and serial licensors. The first licence is the most difficult. Each licence thereafter is likely to be less costly to execute and more productive in operation. Even if professional help is needed to develop the strategy and in drafting the licensing agreements, when licensing in, think business growth strategy!

John D Emanuel is Chairman of Pax Technology Transfer Ltd, past Chairman of the Institute of International Licensing Practitioners. He is Chairman of UTEK-Pax Ltd, formerly Pax Technology Transfer Ltd which he founded in 1978, and Vice-President of UTEK Corporation (US) with which Pax merged in 2001. Pax, which he founded in 1978, specializes in finding technology-driven business opportunities for dynamic companies. UTEK specializes in transferring 'disruptive' technology from research organizations to high-tech companies. Licensing is central to both activities.

For further information contact the Institute of International Licensing Practitioners, Oxford Centre for Innovation, Mill Street, Oxford, OX2 0JX, England; tel: +44(0)1865 812060; fax: +44(0)1865 793265; e-mail: enquiries@iilp.net; Web site: www.iilp.net

Portfolio management

John Lawrence at Barker Brettell discuss how to ensure a portfolio matches current and future needs.

The first thing an organization needs is to know what patents it already has – in other words, to get a schedule. It is surprising how many managers of companies do not actually know what patents they have, or in what countries, or what they cover. Knowing that patents were taken out to cover 'Project Excalibur' is not the same thing as knowing what the patents actually do cover. Do they cover all ways of achieving a particular result, or just one way? Obviously, the broader the scope of protection, the more likely it is that the patent will still have value some years later as other ways of achieving similar effects come to the fore. A patent taken out for 'Project Excalibur' five years ago might also cover 'Project Merlin' now.

So a first exercise is to get a schedule of all of the organization's patents from its patent attorney; either go through the claims at the end of the patent, or get the patent attorney to do it, and write down in a few key words the critical thing that is protected by each patent. (The claims at the end of the patent define the legal protection.)

Next, it is necessary to overlay onto that schedule how much it will cost the organization to keep the patent in force for another year. However, since most patents have an annual renewal fee, it is also worth overlaying on a second version of the schedule how much it will cost to keep the patent in force over the next three years, say. Finally, it is important to decide what type of benefit is being derived from this particular patent, or what benefit the organization could get if it used it properly, and decide whether it is worth keeping it in force.

Historic cost versus future benefit

Some people look at the historic cost of getting the patent in the first place, and maintaining it up until the current date and conclude that compared with that cost, a few hundred pounds to keep it going seems money well spent. My personal view is that this historical value approach roots organizations in the past instead of encouraging them to looking forward.

We are where we are and the questions are, 'Where are we now?' and 'Where do we want to be in a few years' time?'

Obviously, when assessing what value is obtained from a patent it is a good idea for the organization to consider whether it is getting the best value possible out of it. Does it know how to use it in the commercial market place? Do its salespeople know when to mention it? Has it considered licensing it? There can be significant costs in filing a patent or trade mark and taking it forward in other countries, and in pursuing the applications through to grant. Filing a patent application is only the start of the expense. It is important to make sure there is a projected cost schedule.

Making choices

One good way of approaching a patent portfolio is to patent anything that moves in the first place but be ruthless in culling it once it is clear that it is not worth carrying on. Unfortunately, it is far harder to spot the winners and differentiate them from the losers than it is to patent seemingly good ideas.

Most organizations do not have an unlimited budget. Choices need to be made. These choices will depend upon the nature of innovation in the company. If it has produced only one new product in the past 10 years, and does not envisage having another new product for 10 years, it might make more sense to protect the existing product in a wider number of countries, rather than save the budget to protect the next new idea when it comes along. On the other hand, if it has a large portfolio, files 20 new applications a year, and typically carries on activities in five or six overseas countries, it will need to play the percentages and see where to get the best value for its money.

In general, 'translation countries' are more expensive than English-language countries. The United States is the largest market for most things. Europe as a whole is typically the second largest market. There are a lot worse policies than to patent just in the United States and Europe and not worry about other countries. Obviously, each industry is different and each company is different. If the organization's major rivals are in Japan, this will bring forward the importance of Japan. If it is selling solar power equipment perhaps it will really be interested in the Mediterranean countries, the United States and Australia. While there is a lot of sun in Africa, there is not much money for buying equipment.

There are international patent systems (the PCT system) that can keep options open for two and a half years from the first invention, at which point it might be clearer how the project is going and what matters to customers – so attention can be focused on that. The success, or otherwise, of the product internationally might also be clearer then.

Matching the trade mark portfolio to sales in particular countries or to projected sales

It is important to take sales figures by product and country and compare them with the trade mark portfolio. Too many companies have a trade mark portfolio that is based upon the colonial past, which focuses on the Commonwealth, whereas now the company probably trades with Europe more but has not realigned its trade mark portfolio with its trading interest. Right now, many companies have a growing interest in China and India – for the future.

It is true to say that some companies are finding themselves blocked from entering emerging markets because local companies have registered 'their' trade marks ahead of them. Unfortunately, the law of many countries gives no rights just for being famous in the UK – it is more concerned with how famous the name is in that particular country. If a distributor or an ex-distributor registers a trade mark in a particular overseas country, it can be very hard to wrestle it off them. It might be used as leverage by the distributor to persuade the company never to change distributor, irrespective of its performance. Organizations should consider strategic registrations for the future to ensure they are not blocked when the time comes.

Appreciating the value of trade marks

It is easy to see the value of trade marks. No marketing manager will accept the proposition that his or her efforts add no value to the sales of the company. The salaries of the marketing team, the office overheads they use, and the actual marketing spend might amount to £500,000 a year. If they do indeed increase sales/add value, why would the organization not wish to spend money protecting the benefit of that effort?

Over a 10-year period, the marketing spend might be £5 million. There is value in spending that. There should be value in protecting the benefit of that spend. Many trade marks last for 10 years before they need renewing, and since they can be kept in force indefinitely, a ballpark figure of £1,000 from start to finish to register a UK trade mark comes out at £100 a year. Compare this with the £5 million spent and it is a no-brain decision to protect the marks.

There are very good international trade mark schemes which enable organizations to get value for money across a wide number of countries. There is a common European Community trade mark covering the whole of the EU. There is the Madrid Protocol covering 60-plus countries. If the organization has a genuine trading subsidiary in continental Europe, there is also the Madrid Agreement covering even more countries.

A sum of £3,000–4,000 to protect a trade mark across the whole of the EU, now extended to 25 countries, and lasting for 10 years at a time, comes out at less than £20 per country per year to protect whatever value is added by the entire marketing department for a particular brand. If the brand is copied in a particular country in the EU, and if you are the person who decided not to spend £20 per country per year to protect it, you will not be a happy person when the managing director asks to see you.

Differences in approach

There is quite a strong difference in the psychological approaches between managing a trade mark portfolio and a patent portfolio. Patent applications need, as a rule, to be filed while the invention is still secret. There comes a point when it is too late to file patent applications in new countries. On the other hand, it is never too late to file a trade mark application (unless someone else has got there first in a particular country and already registered the mark). There is more scope for increasing the country coverage of a trade mark portfolio after the product has been on the market for some time than there is for increasing the country coverage for patents.

Trade marks tend to have a longer commercial life and perhaps should be thought of as 10- to 50-year property (or longer – the UK's first trade mark registered in 1876, the Bass red triangle, is still registered for beer). Patents last for a maximum of 20 years, and in some technologies are out of date after 10 years. It depends how fast-moving the technology is and how broad the definition of protection in the patent is. Just because a product is out of date does not mean that the patent is not covering new products.

Registered designs

Is the organization registering its designs? Design registration protects the visual appearance of a design. A design-led company which sells things that look good, or are intended to look good, should know about it. The cost is even cheaper than for registering trade marks. Design registration includes a grace period (at least for the EU and the United States, two very important markets). It might cost £1,200 to register a design in the EU (25 countries), and the registration lasts for five years before it needs renewing. This comes to £50 per country per year.

An even better deal can be obtained by saving up designs and registering 10 or 20 every year. The pricing structure of the EU design registration scheme is such that instead of costing 20 times as much as registering one design, it might only cost 5 to 10 times as much.

Questions to ask

- Does the organization use the same patent and trade mark firm to perform renewals as to file and prosecute patents and trade marks? Does it use a separate renewal agency? Is the cost saving really present?
- Should it endorse some of its patent 'licences of right', halving the annual renewal fees?
- Should it use the European Patent Office/Community Trademark Office, or file separate national applications in a few countries?
- Should it rush its patents through to grant within a year or drag them out, spreading the cost over five or six years? (There are pros and cons for both options.)
- Should it treat every patent/trade mark the same? (Answer: no.)
- Does it have an annual in-house lecture from its patent and trade mark attorney on IP, raising awareness of IP, and exposing the IP policy to relevant people within the company?
- Does it have an IP policy written down?
- Does it know who are 'the relevant people' within the organization who need to know what IP it has and how to leverage business with it?

John Lawrence is a leading client development partner at Barker Brettell and is one of the UK's most successful independent patent attorneys. He works from the firm's Birmingham and London offices.

He has 20 years of working with UK companies, and has developed an especially strong interest in the United States. He has lectured the patent profession both in the UK and in the United States, and is one of the more proactive, outgoing, patent attorneys. His achievements range from coming first in the UK in his professional examinations many years ago, to conducting (and winning) the first opposition hearing in the European Patent Office in The Hague, and to maintaining the reputation of the UK patent profession at the Munich Beer Festival on a regular basis.

IP commercialization

Once Head of Technology Transfer at Glasgow University and now CEO of Science Ventures and Chairman of Projected Outcome Ltd, Billy Harkin has learnt that commercializing IP is a team sport.

It has been said that the person who invented the first ever wheel was probably just a lucky fool, but the person who invented the other three was a genius! The point is that it is not so much the invention itself that matters, but whether it is *organized to achieve any useful purpose*. My own example is that it is perfectly possible to take two successful inventions – the helicopter and the lawnmower – and configure them together to produce a flying lawnmower. And because the combination is not obvious (until now) I would even be likely to get a patent granted for it. It would be really funny to watch some lunatic trying to cut the grass with the prototype! However, in the end all the expense of patenting it, getting the project financed and then producing it would all be in vain – simply because the invention in question is clearly a commercial loser. Sadly, 'flying lawnmowers', in the form of similarly commercially stupid inventions, represent the majority of inventions filed, sometimes granted, and always paid for.

There is another school of thought that feels that since we just never know what *might* commercially succeed and what will not, we should patent every flying lawnmower that someone dreams up. For me the choice is not an intellectual one, it is simply a financial one – only the very rich can afford to play that speculative game; and good luck to those that can. That same group can, and does often, afford to gain patent protections simply as a strategic defence measure.

Statistically, making money out of intellectual property (IP) rights, as opposed to solely spending money on them, enjoys a slightly better success probability level than of that of a single sperm. For the majority of people (and organizations), *efficiency* is the key.

'IP commercialization' activity is entirely unregulated, there is no common 'operating system', no quality standard. Each project is 'managed' by whoever shouts loudest or holds strongest control (whether he or she has any talent or not), each project team is typically 'assembled' by osmosis, rather than by design, then this 'team' (which usually no one has told actually is a team) advances along whatever path appears to make best sense on a day-to-day basis. Not surprisingly, the resultant outcome is usually tears and disappointment. Products that could have made money in the market do not get there. Societal benefits that should have been gained were not. And entire industries and regional economies are retarded as a result. It is difficult to overstate the pivotal importance of getting IP commercialization right.

So what are the processes at play, and how does the intrepid IP creator or owner decide what best to do, and when and how to do it? In particular, how do you do it at the lowest possible cost, in the shortest possible time and gain the best possible financial return – generally the main point of the exercise in the first place? That is unless, of course, you can afford to pay for uncommercial patents to be granted just for the ego trip, and have nothing more important to do.

Ownership and protection (a *spending* money activity)

'Inventions' and other protected intellectual property rights have been formally around as protected assets for over 300 years. Pretty much every government in the world by now also adheres to agreed protocols regarding how the ownership-granting system works – and even the cost to the customer of gaining granted ownership rights is becoming better value over time.

Although the actual level of fees charged by the government authorities, the patent offices, are relatively low, the overall process still typically starts off at low cost, get expensive very quickly and is then followed by significant ongoing annual costs. This high jump in cost is caused by the fact that patent lawyers charge like a wounded bull.

These additional costs are entirely optional, but missing them out is a little bit like choosing to buy a house without using a lawyer to ensure that you finally own what you aimed to own: it is perfectly possible to do, but often results in expensive, irreversible regret. In addition to helping people and organizations gain stronger ownership rights in the first place, patent-legal professionals are the folk who will help them defend their position when attacked – and attacked they will be, if there comes to be clear financial value in their position.

As with any professional service there are good patent lawyers and bad ones, so shop around. And remember to shop around for quality of output, rather than for simply the lowest price.

Assembling a commercialization team (a *spending* money activity)

There are only two approaches to making money from IP assets. One involves a lone inventor, from whatever individual background and financial status, personally leading in putting together and executing an effective process that culminates in successful licence deals or the setting up of a new company to produce and then profitably sell products. All and any other outcomes represent 'game over', usually with the inventor having run out of both time and money. Approach number two involves a multidisci-plinary team that collaboratively makes the project a success.

Independent inventors and small companies share certain characteristics. Those few that succeed do so because of the drive and enthusiasm of the people involved, and their success is directly proportional to the performance of the people involved – and key, how well they are coordinated. This people-centric factor is highlighted when we consider what essential skills and resources are required to complement the innovative skills of the inventor. Entrepreneurs, accountants, market researchers, PR consultants, engineers, product designers, recruitment firms, bankers, investors and other expert services all typically play vital roles in getting any invention to market. The team of professionals and functional-specialists that support the inventor must be assembled carefully, then managed ruthlessly and economically. Achieving this is a truly monumental task, and is without doubt the critical failure of the traditional and still current process, or lack thereof.

The main advice here is always recognize that there has never in the history of the world been an invention or other IP asset that succeeded because of the actions of one person alone – it is always a team sport. And the successful ones are the ones that have been well project managed, and are led by an able project manager who understands the entire process (*not* just the product design bit, or the funding bit, or the patenting bit).

Selecting and managing an effective process (the key) to making money

Starting from the team-sport perspective then, and having first generated some IP asset, the next step is to identify the process to be followed – from the IP generation point all the way through to licence deals and/or new company launch. Make sure that a structured process is followed. Next, identify the profile of the team members required for the particular project (which might be a domestic appliance, medical device, computer game or whatever). The next step is to produce a project plan for making it all happen, subject only to finding the money needed. Then, and only then, it is necessary to find the money to breath life into the plan. Do not go messing about producing prototypes as a first and entirely isolated activity!

If it is not possible to find the money to properly play out the structured plan, there are clearly two choices. One is to try to slog it out to a lower standard, taking a dangerously much longer time to market. The second is to remain focused only on finding the money, until it is obtained. I myself have always found enduring the frustration of selecting option two to be the most efficient for any project in the end.

Licence income, product sales income and capital gains (the *making* money activities)

Today, only around 15 per cent of patents filed annually, in either Europe or the United States, receive any commercialization attention at all post their filing. IP asset management requires a lot of consistent attention to make commercial success a reality. Any project truly worth advancing is worth advancing as a full-time endeavour. It is a full-time job.

Once the IP asset has been managed all the way through to a robust demonstrator that has been produced against a demonstrable market need, whether it is a piece of engineered kit, a software item or whatever, the real fun begins. This involves identifying the most suitable companies (as opposed to the first one accidentally bumped into) in the world to sell licences to, then getting the deal done.

If a new company is deemed most suitable as the route to market, again it is important to make sure that the person leading on achieving this has solid experience in successfully setting up new companies, with proper management teams and properly funded. Inventors are notorious for creating half-baked, poorly structured companies that then go on to ruin wonderful and valuable inventions.

Summary

IP commercialization is complex, difficult, frustrating, expensive, and seldom delivers success. It is great fun, though – and when it does deliver success, it changes the world and there is no other business success quite like it! It is not an ad hoc process – it is a professional one. Get organized, assemble a team, select a process – 'EIPAM or equivalent – and execute effectively on your plan.

Billy Harkin is CEO of Science Ventures and Chairman of Projected Outcome Ltd. His knowledge and experience has been gained over 22 years from not only being an inventor himself, but also being the former head of Technology Transfer at the University of Glasgow, Scotland and driving that campus to a top profile in the UK for its commercialization success during his tenure. Billy also drew from experiences gained during his time spent in Europe, Asia, Africa and the United States, benchmarking IP management and commercialization strategies and execution techniques. He has also been influenced by experiences gained starting and running technology and marketing companies. Finally, his portfolio includes influences gained during a period within Scotland's economic development agency's Technology Ventures initiative.

Billy is a regular speaker at IP commercialization 'best practice' events globally. The EIPAM application is based on a methodology and toolset devised by the author.

For further information contact: bharkin@projected-outcome. com and bharkin@scienceventures.com

A falling apple inspired Newton...

No matter what inspires you, we can help you to obtain the best value from your ideas.

Trade Marks
Copyright
Design Rights
Watching services
Expert Witness services

The Law Society of Scotland
2004
Directory of Expert Witnesses

Patents
Registered Designs
Domain names
Search services

Fitzpatricks®

chartered patent attorneys
trade mark attorneys

4 West Regent Street - Glasgow - G2 1RS **T:** 0141 306 9000 **F:** 0141 306 9090 **E:** POH@fitzpatricks.co.uk
W: www.fitzpatricks.co.uk

3
IP in the growth cycle

London innovation

LONDON DEVELOPMENT AGENCY

Fresh thinking for

better business

How can you grow in a competitive world? What will increase your productivity? Who can give you the advice to turn new ideas to business advantage?

Tap into London's knowledge base with London Innovation. London Innovation exists to help London's businesses grow. We can help inspire your enterprise.

To find out more, visit:
www.london-innovation.org.uk
London innovation – turning bright ideas into business success.

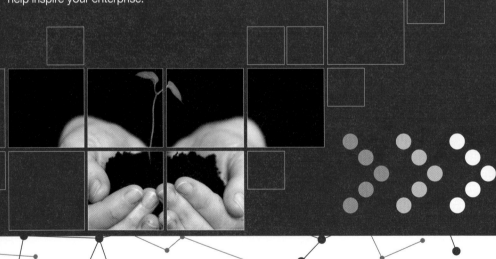

www.**london-innovation**.org.uk

Invention to business

Having a great idea is not enough to make a great business, says Linda Oakley at ideas 21.

It all sounds so simple, so straightforward, so effortless.... A flash of inspiration and a great idea becomes a household name and makes millions. But the reality is rarely so simple. Ideas might be relatively easy to come by, but too often first-time inventors confuse an 'idea' with an invention – the technical application of an idea to provide a new product or process. Turning an invention into a profitable business is an altogether different matter.

Thousands of inventors and innovators file for patents each year, and it is estimated that only 1 in 100 will cover costs and only 1 in 1,400 becomes a world-beater. Once a patent has been filed, the clock starts to tick away, leaving only 12 months to decide if protection is to be applied for in other countries outside the UK. Remember that it takes knowledge, time, money and effort to refine an idea into a workable invention, even on paper. Turning that invention into a new product accepted by the marketplace is even harder.

The market

Obtaining a patent for an invention will not generate any income if it is for a product that no one will want or can afford to buy. Identifying the market for an invention is crucial for success; a business can fail if unrealistic market research has been undertaken or if the findings have been interpreted too optimistically.

The competition

Is there anything similar on the market and what advantages will the new invention give? There might simply not be enough demand for a new or modified feature to an existing product, and it is therefore pointless proceeding with the whole of the invention.

Finding out as much about the competition as possible will also give an understanding of that industry, if it is in decline or if growth conditions require a different approach.

Just because a product is new does not always mean the market will welcome it. People are reluctant to change, and established companies have spent years and hundreds of thousands of pounds ensuring that their products remain on the shelves.

The right price

However much people might like an idea, the price must be right, affordable to the consumer and make a commercial return for the business. An invention aimed at a low-volume, low-profit market could mean expenditure is too high for a business to be sustainable. High-volume, low-profit-margin markets can however bring success.

John Osher, an American entrepreneur, tapped into a market with his SpinBrush, the first low-cost, mass-marketed mechanical toothbrush. At around US $80 each an electric toothbrush was too expensive for many buyers; at under US $5 it became not only affordable to a bigger market, but also a product that people would buy again and again. In 2001 John Osher sold the SpinBrush to Procter & Gamble for US $475 million.

> Our advantage was that we were trying to design up from 80 cents, while everybody else was trying to design down from $79.
>
> John Osher

Does the invention work?

A business will be short-lived if it is built around an invention that does not work or does not meet a customer's needs or expectations. Making a prototype will ensure that an idea actually works, and identifies technical problems. It could mean going back to the drawing board, making changes as needed, testing and retesting to get the bugs out. Refining an invention from paper to a workable model can take time. James Dyson made 5,127 prototypes over five years before perfecting his vacuum cleaner.

Designing an invention

Design is often seen as an afterthought, but it is a vital connection between prototyping and manufacturing. An invention can often be hidden by poor design. A good design can affect the cost of manufacturing the invention in volume, for example by optimizing the type of material that it will be made from and how the invention is used. In today's consumer market functionality alone is not always enough to encourage people to buy the product.

Manufacturing an invention

The difference between an idea and a product is manufacturing. A great idea makes no money until it is produced and sold in multiple units at a realistic price. Understanding the options available of how an idea can be manufactured can affect budget and therefore the sale price. Maintaining quality is a large factor in the long-term success of a product. As the idea is engineered for manufacturing, new ways may be found to patent and protect it.

Same invention – different market

An invention may offer a solution to a certain problem but a new, unforeseen market can open up. A university research chemist was working on some hydrogels – polymeric materials that absorb many times their own weight of water causing them to swell, for instance from a small amount of dry whitish powder to a big pile of translucent gel material. The results were encouraging, and proposed uses for this curious material were imagined. One was to close an irrigation valve by blocking it with the swollen hydrogel. When the hydrogel dried out, it shrank and opened the valve to let more water on to the crops, and on to the hydrogel, so it expanded again and closed off the flow. This was very automatic and labour-saving.

A more ingenious proposal was for treating animals such as cows. The hydrogel, including a drug, was put in a mesh bag small enough for the cow to swallow. Once swallowed, the hydrogel expanded on contact with the fluid in the cow's stomach, so preventing the now inflated bag getting any further than the cow's first stomach. The drug was gradually released and the hydrogel dissolved – so after a few weeks of treatment, the cow was better and the now reduced-size bag was able to pass through the remainder of its digestive system.

Another use for the hydrogels turned out to be much simpler and for quite a different market: mixing the hydrogels into the soil round a potted houseplant. Before the owner goes away on holiday, the soil can be overwatered, and the hydrogels absorb the excess and swell. As the plant uses up the water, more is released from the hydrogel, keeping the plant watered.

Costs

Everything costs. There is a certain amount of free advice available but when starting a business, sufficient capital is essential. Many inventors are able to be successful in business by licensing their invention. If the invention works, can be manufactured at the right price, and has a potential market, this knowledge can make it easier to license the idea. An established company that is au fait with the market and has existing distribution channels can succeed a lot quicker than an individual with no experience. Even with massive infusions of cash, some ideas cannot make it in today's market.

In business there are no guarantees, and overcoming these substantial barriers requires careful planning to control costs and limit risks.

The team

Successful businesses are born out of inventions: look around and you will see there is still plenty of room for the world to embrace something new. People do not realize how life-changing an invention can be until they start to use it, then they find they would not be without it. One of the most important ingredients to success is the perseverance, determination and foresight of the individual who surrounds him- or herself with the correct team that can turn an invention into a successful business.

Linda Oakley is co-founder of ideas 21 and chair of Women in Invention and Innovation. For further information tel: +44 (0) 20 7242 3094; www.ideas21.co.uk

protecting ideas so they flourish

- One of Europe's largest and fastest growing Attorney practices

- 140 people in seven offices in six European countries

- Seamless client representation at the European, UK, Irish, French and Dutch Patent Offices, and the Community Trade Mark Office

- 50 technical staff covering all technical fields

- Focus on service delivery and response times

- Simple, transparent pricing

- Effective relations with other professionals

- Experienced in IP due diligence

- In-house Patent and Trade Mark searchers

- In-house technical illustrators

- In-house technical translators

- 3D modelling and virtual prototyping service

www.murgitroyd.com

email: **mail@murgitroyd.com**

UK Offices ;

Glasgow
Scotland House
165-169 Scotland Street
Glasgow
G5 8PL
T 0141-307 8400
F 0141-307 8401

Aberdeen
Exploration House
Exploration Drive
Aberdeen
AB23 8GX
T 01224- 706 616
F 01224- 706 617

Belfast
Clarence Chambers
18 Donegall Square East
Belfast
BT1 5HE
T 028- 9032 0441
F 028- 9032 0442

Other offices in
Dublin, London, Nice & Munich

Implications of trading on the Web

A distinctive name for a Web site is easier to protect if it can be registered as a trade mark, says Stephen Kinsey at Wildbore & Gibbons.

Choosing a domain name

As the Web evolves, there is a growing expectation among potential customers that a company's Web site address will contain its trade mark, or at least reflect its 'corporate identity'. For one thing, such a Web site is generally easier to find. If you want to visit Aviva plc's Web site to check out its insurance deals, for example, keying in www.aviva.com is a better bet than trawling through search engine references to 'insurance'.

Of course, there is nothing wrong with using a generic (descriptive) term as your Internet address, and many larger companies will register as domain names, names and phrases that describe their goods and services, as well as their trade marks. But the lack of distinctiveness in a descriptive word might mean that, as a small or medium-sized enterprise (SME), you need to register dozens of variants as domain names in order to protect your position. Many businesses now find themselves burdened with very long lists of domain names to renew and maintain, most of which they will never use. For this reason, the SME is best advised to give priority to its trade marks when registering domain names.

Pick a distinctive name

A thorough trade mark search for an organization starting out in business, or choosing a new brand, will always include a search among domain names. It might be better to choose a new trade mark rather than continue with one that cannot be used as part of a .com or .co.uk domain name because someone else has reserved it. A distinctive name for a domain is easier to protect if it can be registered as a trade mark.

Reserve possible domain names first

A medium-sized or large public limited company, perhaps about to rebrand or merge, will find it best to reserve a potential domain name before it has completed its trade mark clearance searches. Certainly it should make appropriate reservations before it makes an announcement about the name to the press or its workforce. If security is an issue, it is possible to arrange to register a domain name through an agent who has agreed to transfer the domain to the organization when the new trade mark is announced.

Consider trade mark registration early on

Any distinctive domain name reservation is potentially a global brand. When a Web site and e-mail address are established, enquiries may reach them from all over the world. Even if the organization is not initially able to supply customers from all over the world, it must first protect its trade mark rights. The priority is probably the home market. If the organization has chosen a distinctive domain name to be its trade mark, a United Kingdom trade mark registration will not only enable it to prevent others using the same or a similar mark, but can also provide:

- a defence to a claim of infringement of any other party's trade mark rights in the United Kingdom;
- a priority period (six months) for applying for registration overseas;
- a good basis for objecting to other domain name reservations.

Use and police the domain name properly

Consider including an indication on the Web site that the domain name is a registered trade mark in the United Kingdom and any other jurisdictions, along with any standard notices the Web site designer may recommend relating to a prohibition on copying. In addition to subscribing to a reputable trade mark watching service, it is also advisable to arrange regular checks of Internet search engines for metatags and banners using the trade mark.

Protecting a domain name trade mark

Although a domain name registration is not in itself an IP right, it has some of the characteristics of an exclusive right because of its uniqueness within a top-level domain (TLD). There are generic TLDs (gTLDs), such as .com, .org and .net, and country code TLDs (ccTLDS), such as .co.uk. A domain name can exist only once within one TLD, while similar trade marks can be used by organizations in different fields, so companies that have by coincidence chosen the same name for their trade mark for different products and services might nonetheless find themselves in competition to secure corresponding domain name rights.

Moreover, ever since the commercial potential of the Web became a reality, trade marks have attracted cybersquatters. These are persons or companies without a legitimate interest in a trade mark, who secure the domain name and seek (either actively or passively) to sell the relevant contractual rights with the registration authority to the anxious trade mark owner. There is nothing to stop cybersquatting, or something very like it, being conducted on an industrial scale, with hundreds of trade marks or potential trade marks being reserved as domain names to one company.

Settling domain name disputes

Companies that have the same name by coincidence are often able to settle their differences through their trade mark attorneys. Trade mark coexistence or 'delineation' agreements are a well-established feature of the IP landscape, and are often now adapted to cover Internet issues. Parties can, for example, agree to share a one-page Web site which then points the enquirer to the company Web site of the enquirer's choice.

As to dealing with cybersquatters or other hostile domain name owners, the trade mark owner's only recourse at first (apart from buying out the other party) was to the courts. Litigation is notoriously an expensive and time-consuming process, and by the late 1990s there were so many domain name disputes that the US government-backed Internet Corporation for Assigned Names and Numbers (ICANN) adopted a Uniform Domain Name Dispute Resolution Policy (UDRP). This was originally established to deal with disputes in the gTLDs, but has now been adopted by over 30 ccTLDs. Its intention has always been to resolve only clear-cut cases of cybersquatting or similar problems. It works like this:

When a domain name is registered, the registrant is bound by an agreement with ICANN to submit to the terms of the UDRP. This means that if there is a complaint from a trade mark owner, the registration can be cancelled or transferred if it is shown that the domain name is 'abusive'. Under the UDRP, this requires the trade mark owner to show not only that the domain name is identical or confusingly similar to the trade mark, but also that the domain name holder has no right or legitimate interest in the name, and that it was registered and is used in bad faith. Trade mark owners have sometimes found all these conditions difficult to prove. There is however no doubt that the procedure is very successful, with less than 1 per cent of all disputes continuing in the courts after the UDRP has been followed.

In the United Kingdom, the ccTLD authority, Nominet, has adopted its own dispute resolution policy. Instead of having to show registration and use in bad faith, the complainant has to show that the domain name registration and/or use takes unfair advantage of, or is unfairly detrimental to, the complainant's rights. This is intended to allow, within the law, for 'tribute' and 'criticism' Web sites to use the trade marks of others in their Internet addresses.

Metatags

Apart from cybersquatting, the other major issue for trade mark owners is usually the use by competitors of their trade marks in Web site metatags. Metatags by definition are tags buried in the software making up a Web page, which are not visible on the user's computer screen but which are picked up by search engines.

The English Court of Appeal ruled earlier this year that the services of a competitor would have to be identical if the trade mark owner was to have a clear-cut action for infringement. If the services were only similar it would be necessary to show a likelihood of confusion. As a result, the Reed Employment Group was unable to prevent the Reed Elsevier publishing group from using 'Reed' as a metatag on its Web site, or from reserving 'Reed' as a banner advertisement key word on a proprietary search engine.

Libel on the Internet

Trade mark attorneys have long been familiar with the notion of 'trade libel'. From time to time, a trader may be inclined to make malicious and defamatory statements about a competitor's products or services, and to identify those products or services by using the relevant trade mark. There are of course industry codes covering advertising standards, the best known being that of the Advertising Standards Authority, but occasionally the matter can come to court. When a party is libelled on the Internet, the question arises where the libel has been committed. The English High Court regards Internet material as being published where it is downloaded. Thus, if a trade libel on a Web site is accessed by customers in England, the libel will have occurred in England.

The safest rule? Do not refer to a competitor's trade mark on a Web site unless you are confident that the statements or comparisons you are making can be shown to be both true and fair.

Stephen Kinsey has a Master's degree in European Union Commercial Law and is a Fellow of the Institute of Trade Mark Attorneys. Wildbore & Gibbons is the longest-established independent firm of trade mark attorneys in the United Kingdom, and specializes in the protection of brands through trade mark and design registration. For further information contact: info@wildbore.co.uk

Invention promotion companies

David Wardell, Chairman of the Institute of Patentees and Inventors, on the pros and cons of invention promotion companies.

Ah … the vexed question of invention promotion companies. Often compared to vanity publishing, some demonize them, others eulogize. I have met people who are very happy with the service they received and others who are very disgruntled. What's the truth?

It is important to understand what an invention promotion company is. The premise is very simple. In return for a fee, a promoter will attempt to find a commercial partner for an invention. Some offer other services such as market research and improved presentation materials. Some have large databases from which they organize mail-outs to potentially interested parties. Very few of these companies work in partnership with the inventor – everything is fee-based.

Lots have come and gone over the years. Some are home-grown, more usually they are based in the United States, but there are also a few in the Far East. Some work by word of mouth and others engage in high-profile advertising campaigns. Some are large organizations and others are 'one man bands'. They strive to do the same thing, namely to put their clients' inventions in front of those who can take them forward commercially.

So, why does such a simple business model give rise to much argument and polarization within the international inventor community? Essentially there are two bones of contention. First, rarely does an invention promoter vet or assess the commercial worth of the inventions presented to it. Second, they have low success rates in actually making money for their clients. I have some sympathy with both arguments.

I have questioned invention promoters as to why they do not assess inventions, and the answer is very simple. They do not feel that it is their job, because if the inventor truly believes in the idea, it is up to them how they attempt to bring it to market. From my own point of view, I can confirm that it is very difficult to assess the worth of an invention. In this business there are many examples of inventors being told that their idea was going nowhere who have then gone on to prove their detractors spectacularly wrong. Conversely, over the years I have seen many inventions that on the face of it had bright futures, but failed to get to market for all sorts of unexpected reasons. Therefore an invention promoter would look fairly silly if it turned away clients who went on to be successful, and it cannot be expected to second guess whether a potentially good idea will fail for unexpected reasons. This is a form of Catch 22. There is also the problem of the inventors themselves. Every inventor is convinced that his or her idea is 'the one' and will brook no criticism.

As far as low success rates are concerned, I can only say that I am not surprised. Unfortunately, low success rates go with the territory. It is a sad fact that only 3–5 per cent of inventions patented by individuals ever make it to market. Add to this the fact that there is no assessment of the invention, and some invention promoters' figures begin to look quite reasonable. A reputable invention promotion company will warn the inventor that his or her chances of success are slim. It will also provide a contract which gives the inventor the opportunity to really think about what he or she is doing before signing on the dotted line. A 'cooling-off' period should be provided.

Inventors really need to think about whether using the services of a promoter is the right approach for them. If the inventor is the sort of person who wants to be involved with every stage and negotiation of the commercialization process, and actively wants to go out to promote the invention, then this route is probably not the right one. In talking to some American inventors I have noticed a few cultural differences in approach. Many US inventors have stated that they 'had a bit of an idea' which they wanted to do something about. It is almost an itch that must be scratched. However, they are so busy in getting on with their normal lives and careers that they cannot take the time out to work on their invention. These people are money rich but time poor. In this case they use the services of an invention promoter, taking the view that for a fixed fee someone else does all the work. If the invention goes on to be successful, that is great. If it fails, at least they tried.

A few practices give me some cause for concern. Anyone entering into a contract with a company that has a UK office has some protection through the Trading Standards Office. However, I am aware of one company that routes telephone enquiries to another EU country which are then re-routed to the United States. This company gives the impression that it is UK-based, but it is actually outside any UK jurisdiction. Another practice that appears somewhat underhand is to advertise services under the guise of 'help lines' or the promise of 'information packs'. This gives the impression that it is information from some sort of government agency or inventor organization, rather than for the sale of commercial services.

Is it all bad? No, of course not. Some companies have dramatically improved their services in recent years, with the provision of real information about success rates, and much improved contracts that give the correct warnings and allow potential clients to review their options. I have met dedicated and enthusiastic people who do their best to promote their clients' interests and ensure that they satisfy any contractual agreements.

The Patent Office has issued a set of guidelines to help inventors decide whether using an invention promoter is right for them. Taken individually these guidelines make good sense; however, collectively they might seem a little draconian.

The Patent Office's step-by-step guide to using invention promoters

- Do you think you have a great idea for a new product or service? You are not alone.
- Every year thousands of people try to develop their ideas and market them commercially. Some people use the services of invention promotion firms to help evaluate, develop and market their idea. Contracting for the services of such firms is no different from making any other major purchase. If you are interested in working with one, before entering into a contract, the following common sense guidance may help you to avoid costly mistakes.
- Do your homework – there is a considerable amount of free or low-cost advice available, on issues such as patenting and other forms of intellectual property protection, which you may wish to consider first. A few of these sources or routes to information are suggested below.
- Do not disclose the details of your invention to anyone, including the promoter, without a prior confidentiality agreement. Failure to keep the details private could prevent you from obtaining intellectual property rights in the future.
- Early in your discussion with a promotion firm, find out exactly what the different stages of the service are and the costs associated

with each stage, from the 'research' about your invention right through to the marketing and licensing.

- Ask the firm to provide evidence that it has the necessary skills and expertise in the field of your interest to support the activities that they agree to carry out on your behalf.
- Ask what success rate the firm has achieved in promoting inventions since it started offering its services, and find out whether references can be provided from recent clients.
- Question claims and assurances that your invention will make money. Commercialization of inventions is a risky business – no one can guarantee that your invention will be commercially successful.
- Ask the firm for its rejection rate – the percentage of all ideas or inventions that the invention firm finds unacceptable at the first assessment stage. Not all ideas could be considered to be commercially viable, and it should be expected that firms have high rejection rates.
- Find out whether the services advertised, for example the patent search and/or market assessment, will be carried out in the countries in which you would like to exploit your invention.
- If the invention promotion firm claims to know, or have special access to, manufacturers who are likely to be interested in licensing your invention, or if it claims to represent manufacturers on the look-out for new product ideas, ask for proof.
- If the firm offers the services of a 'patent agent' or 'patent attorney', ask if those people are registered. The Chartered Institute of Patent Agents (CIPA) is the professional body for patent agents in the UK. It aims to increase awareness and understanding of the innovation process by providing a basic information pack and free clinics, and by arranging talks or seminars when appropriate. CIPA members help inventors to obtain protection, not only in patents, but also in trade marks, designs and copyright. For further information call CIPA on +44 (0)20 7405 9450, e-mail mail@cipa.org.uk, or visit its Web site at http://www.cipa.org.uk.
- If the firm offers search services to assess patent prospects, make sure that the search is comprehensive and covers all published prior art. A patent must be new, and if the idea is published anywhere in the world before filing, this will invalidate rights. Compare the cost and thoroughness of the search with that provided by the UK Patent Office.
- If at the end of all this you are happy with the evidence and do wish to enter into a contract, ensure that it contains all the terms you agreed to – verbal and written – before you sign. If possible you should seek legal advice.

There are many ways to take an invention forward to commercialization. There is no definitive correct way, just a series of options. Maybe the services of an invention promoter would be right for you.

David Wardell is the Chairman of the Institute of Patentees and Inventors (IPI). Established in 1919, the IPI has been offering advice and information to inventors for over 80 years (www.invent.org.uk). David is a former Trustee of Nesta – the National Endowment for Science, Technology and the Arts. He is currently a committee member for Nesta's Invention and Innovation programme. He is also the editor and publisher of *IVT* magazine, which provides news and information for inventors, innovators and investors.

Potts, Kerr & Co.

CHARTERED PATENT ATTORNEYS
EUROPEAN PATENT ATTORNEYS
TRADE MARK ATTORNEYS

PATENTS
TRADE MARKS
DESIGNS & COPYRIGHT

Overview
Potts, Kerr & Co. are an established firm of Patent and Trade Mark Attorneys, based in the North West of England, who serve a broad UK and international client base.

Brief History
Established as Potts & Co. in the late 1950's as a continuation of the long established Liverpool based practice of Aloysius J. Davies, Potts & Co. took over the firm of George Ham & Partners, incorporating Harris & Mills (established 1866), and the firm of Browne & Co. (established 1840). The present name was adopted in 1966.

Potts, Kerr & Co. currently have three partners and three technical assistants with a support staff of over 20 handling translation, record keeping, accounts and general office duties.

Range of Client Service
Our practice covers the full range of Intellectual property rights available in United Kingdom, Europe and elsewhere. **Potts, Kerr & Co.** enjoy an international reputation, representing primarily corporate clients, including multinational companies, drawn mainly from America, Europe and Japan and we have an extensive network of associates throughout the world. However, we devote equal attention and importance to the individual inventor and small company.

Patents
As Patent Attorneys, **Potts, Kerr & Co.** have qualified specialists in the mechanical, chemical, biotech, electrical and electronic fields. We are qualified representatives able to prosecute patent applications before the United Kingdom Patent Office and before the European Patent Office. We also handle prosecution and maintenance of patents in most other countries through our network of associates. We offer a range of searching and watching services and can advise and act in respect of general licensing, assignment, and infringement matters.

Trade Marks
Potts, Kerr & Co. are also Trade Mark Attorneys qualified to advise on all aspects of trade mark and service mark law and practice, including the provision of pre-filing and infringement clearance searches and registrability opinions. We file and prosecute Registered Trade Mark applications before the United Kingdom Trade Marks Registry and before the European Office for Harmonisation in the Internal Market (OHIM) for Community Trade Marks. We are further able to prosecute applications for International Registration under the Madrid Protocol.

Designs and Copyright
Potts, Kerr & Co. also have wide experience in the filling and prosecution of applications for UK and Community Design Registrations and can advise fully on Copyright and Design Right related matters.

15 Hamilton Square
Birkenhead, Merseyside CH48 7ED
Web: www.pottskerr.co.uk

Tel: 0151-647-6746
Fax: 0151-647-6158
E-mail: ip@pottskerr.co.uk

Consultation Facilities at Chester and Warrington

University spin-outs

IP can make or break a spin-out, says Dr David Secher of the University of Cambridge.

Spin-out companies have been a high-profile phenomenon of the UK university scene for the past decade. This chapter summarizes some of the issues that have arisen, and covers both strategic and practical points to consider.

Universities have been a source of new companies for more than a hundred years. In the 19th century instrumentation companies were set up in Cambridge to manufacture equipment for scientific research. (University publishing companies go back much further, but some of the oldest remain an integral part of the university, rather than a separate company.) Recently (since 1980 in the United States and since mid-1990s in the UK), universities have taken a much more active interest in intellectual property, asserting ownership rights and consequently playing a more active role in developing spin-outs.

In the United States the term 'spin-out' is largely unused. The equivalent companies there are called 'start-ups'. This latter term is used in the UK too, but here it is used to describe a different type of company. In UK English, a spin-out is a company that is founded on intellectual property arising out of research in the university. Normally the university will own shares in a spin-out, and the spin-out will have attracted capital investment. 'Start-ups' in UK parlance are other companies set up by university staff or students (or sometimes alumni) that do not meet the above criteria. These include consultancy businesses and other businesses unrelated to research in the university. This transatlantic difference in the use of language is the source of much confusion! I shall use the British usage throughout this chapter.

In North America more than 4,500 new spin-out companies have been recorded in surveys carried out since 1980 by the Association of University Technology Managers (AUTM). In the UK around 140 have been identified in each of the past two years, according to surveys initiated by UNICO and carried out last year in partnership with Nottingham University Business School and AURIL. The UK achievement is small compared with North America, but when normalized to GDP, or to research expenditure in universities, the number of spin-outs exceeds that of the United States. This simple comparison, together with a political belief that the number of spin-outs is a good surrogate marker of wealth creation, has provided the basis for much attention in, and media reporting of, the activity.

High media profile and government encouragement are two of the factors that have stimulated universities to spin out more and more companies. The extent of university involvement varies greatly. Some universities passively allow new companies to form, then transfer technology to spin-outs much as they would to an existing large company. Others play a crucial role in the founding, investing and directing of spin-outs. The important decisions of how and when to spin out companies should be part of the IP strategy of a university. For some the attraction is the huge profits made by investors in some university spin-outs in the late 1990s. Since then, however, valuations of many spin-outs have fallen dramatically, and licensing to an established business might be less risky and more profitable.

Typical reasons for spinning out a company include a failure to license (is this a disruptive technology unrecognized by the established players?); an inventor who is determined to have his or her own company; a platform technology which needs developing and then has the potential for broad licensing to many companies; and as an incubator for technology that needs further development – beyond the resources of the university environment – before being licensed. Although the prospect of financial return is attractive, the strategic question should be, 'Is this the best way of bringing the benefits of this new technology to a wider society?'

The legal process of spinning out a company is much more complicated – and expensive – than licensing or assigning IP to existing firms. In North America it seems to be less expensive, perhaps through a greater use of standard agreements.

These agreements usually include a 'term sheet' summarizing the key financial and other terms. The term sheet often provides a period of exclusivity during which only a single investor, or syndicate of investors, can investigate in detail the business case ('due diligence'). A key part of due diligence for spin-outs is clarifying the ownership of the intellectual property. This will usually be determined by university rules and contracts of employment, but there may be complications where students are inventors on patents; where the research was sponsored by a third party and the agreement gave the third party some IP rights; or where materials used in making the invention were obtained in return for giving away some IP rights. A smooth deal is much more likely to result if these questions have all been asked – and answered – by the university, before the investors discover problems during due diligence!

Other agreements may include the Memorandum and Articles of Association; consultancy or service contracts; investment agreements; and licence or assignment of IP. Legal and tax advice should be taken by the university and independent advice by the founders – even if they are university employees. There is potential for streamlining this process by developing standard forms of legal agreements.

Whereas most universities have standard arrangements for sharing revenues derived from licensing IP, attempts to standardize the arrangements for sharing equity (shares) in spin-outs have usually failed, because the relative contribution of the inventors, other founders, investors and university varies so widely. It is helpful in negotiating shares in a spin-out to try to recognize separately: contributions for founding the company, rewarding past IP being put into the company, future management or technical input into the company, and investment (even where some of these are provided by a single person). The only non-negotiable rule is that the total must not exceed 100 per cent! University involvement may vary from a passive licensing of IP into a spin-out to an active role through business planning, investment raising or active membership of the board of directors of the spin-out. Universities need to have policies and procedures to support both motivated and skilful entrepreneur inventors (and not get in their way), but also to be able to bring in experienced management to develop technology where the inventor does not want to – or does not have the ability to – get involved with the running of the company.

Money for spin-outs is usually from venture capital firms or wealthy individuals ('business angels'). For the past five years many UK spin-outs have been funded from University Challenge Funds, a very effective DTI initiative.

The past couple of years have seen a decline in the number of UK spin-outs created. This is due to the general investment climate and appetite for early stage investment; uncertainty about how changes in the tax laws affect university staff as founders; and the pendulum swinging back in favour of licensing to established companies, following the failure of some spin-outs to develop university technology by not being able to raise sufficient finance. Spin-outs remain, however, an exciting and important alternative which is here to stay. Preparation, careful planning and good advice will increase the chances of a successful venture.

Dr David Secher is Director of Research Services, University of Cambridge, is a member of the board of UNICO and the Chairman of Praxis Courses. For further information contact: david.secher@rsd.cam.ac.uk

Corporate venturing

Exploiting legacy IP? Managing R&D risk? Julian Wheatland, Corporate Development Director at Edengene, explains how best to capitalize on the potential of corporate venturing.

As corporates strive for growth and new sources of value creation, in an increasingly competitive world, many are turning to their legacy IP portfolios as an asset base for exploitation. This innovative, even entrepreneurial, approach to developing new business activities is often termed corporate venturing.

What corporate venturing is

Corporate venturing can mean many different things depending on the approach being taken, but broadly, corporate venturers divide into two camps: those that invest *externally* in independent, early-stage, IP-rich companies, and those that invest *internally* in creating new businesses from under-utilized assets. The objectives of pursuing corporate venturing initiatives can vary, but both approaches give rise to ventures that will normally enjoy a strategic and competitive advantage over independent market players. There tend to be two main types of corporate objective: strategic enhancement and value creation.

Figure 3.5.1 shows the relationship between different objectives and approaches employed by corporates.

Rationale for Corporate Venture Investment

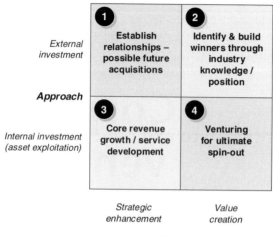

Figure 3.5.1 Rationale for corporate venture investment

Internally focused corporate venturers aim to find new ways to exploit and utilize their IP and assets to create new business propositions. In core markets, these new propositions are strategic and represent top-line revenue growth. In non-core markets, the propositions are less strategic and more about creating valuable new ventures that may, eventually, be spun out.

The rationale for external corporate venture investing is more confused. Many corporates simply aim to identify and create a relationship with early-stage companies that have a technology, or some other intellectual property, that is of strategic interest for the future. The initial investment is generally a minority position, but if things go well they may ultimately seek to take full control. Others have developed a corporate venture-capital investor role, because they believe that their insider industry knowledge enables them to better identify potential winners, and that business synergies can help deliver success.

Of course, there are always exceptions; there being as many variations of corporate venturing as there are corporate venturers. For example, Intel has primarily supported innovative new ventures for strategic reasons: to build new companies that will drive demand for its own products (that is, to stimulate demand for increased processing power). Additionally, it has been shameless about allowing its investees to piggyback off its industry position and relationships! However, it has always aimed to apply the rigorous disciplines of a financial investor to its portfolio, and claims that no conflict of objectives exists.

Whether the focus is internal or external investment, it is to be recognized that a corporate venture has many advantages over an independent venture and as such, has a lower operational risk profile. Corporate investors bring more than just money. Some of the greatest value from a corporate partner is the access to industry knowledge and relationships, sales and marketing support, technology sharing and brand association; and maybe even a ready-made market. These intangible benefits can create significant competitive advantage, substantially increasing the likelihood of venture success.

Corporate venturing to exploit IP

In the context of exploiting and managing IP, both externally and internally focused corporate venturing have important applications.

The pharmaceutical and biotech industry is a clear example of a sector that has virtually reorganized itself along external corporate venturing lines for the purposes of managing R&D risk. In this industry, much of the leading-edge R&D is now undertaken by independent start-ups, which then develop a corporate venturing relationship with pharmaceutical giants (often leading to full acquisition) once the technology is proven.

So the external investment approach to corporate venturing can be seen as an efficient and balanced-risk model of gaining access to new IP and technology. This type of investment stake can be structured to enable a corporate to become familiar with the technology, and allow access to corporate resources to help develop markets, but at the same time remain at arm's length until value is proven.

The internal investment approach to corporate venturing has become popular over recent years, as a means of exploiting legacy IP and technology for new applications. Many companies have found that decades of investing in R&D have yielded a wide range of technologies that could have valuable new applications in both core and non-core markets. However, there are numerous challenges associated with identifying, and capturing, the value embedded in these legacy IP assets. Some of these difficulties, and strategies for managing them, are discussed below.

A practical approach to commercializing legacy IP

IP is a wide term covering tangible and intangible, tacit and implicit intellectual assets. At the heart of creating valuable exploitation routes for legacy IP is the art of innovation: thinking creatively about the assets, assessing new markets, questioning current solutions, challenging traditional thinking and developing new business models. Nevertheless, innovation is only half the story: implementation is where most new business initiatives fail, and where great care needs to be taken if true value is to be created. Set out below is a simple six-stage process that will help organize the work necessary to commercialize legacy IP.

1   Identification

One of the most challenging aspects of the process of harnessing the embedded value in IP is the question of how to identify what the organization has! Corporate IP tends to fall into one of four categories: brands, data, technology and know-how. Brands and data are clearly identifiable assets, but technology and know-how will be distributed across the following three classifications:

■ recognized and patented;
■ recognized and unpatented;
■ unrecognized.

Different approaches and techniques will need to be employed to unearth valuable IP, depending on the category being examined. Patented IP, which by definition has already been recognized as distinct and potentially valuable, can quite easily be mined using one of the commercially available patent data management and analysis tools.

Identifying IP that is unpatented requires a more interactive approach: structured interviews with managers and engineers can be employed to identify IP that has been previously recognized as distinct, but unrecognized IP will probably require a workshop-based approach.

2   Targeting

Targeting is a filtering process. In large organizations where there may be many thousands of distinct technologies and patents, it is necessary to quickly identify the technology domains where there appears to be a high degree of competitive differentiation.

One technique for identifying natural clusters of technologies, and in particular technologies that have proved to be of interest to other organizations, is patent and citation analysis using Micropatent's Aureka software. The themescape function of this software will enable the user to quickly get a picture of the patent portfolio and the natural technology groupings.

This technique can be used to identify 'domains of excellence', even if the ultimate IP to be commercialized is unpatented.

3 Technology assessment and proposition development

Assessing the attractiveness of the technology means understanding the market where it is believed there is a new application. The trick is to gather enough data and analysis to be confident that, not only does a market really exist, but there is sufficient value attached to it to justify commercialization.

The types of question that will need answering are:

- What is the application market size?
- What are the market growth prospects?
- What are the competing solutions?
- How unique is the technology?
- What is the potential number of customers and end-users?
- What is the remaining time to get to market?
- What additional investment will be required?
- How many distinct applications are there?

4 Business model development

Corporate venturing is one model for commercializing technology, but it is not the only route. Once a particular technology application has been identified that looks attractive, the following business models should be considered thoroughly:

- sale of the IP;
- licensing;
- joint venturing;
- corporate venturing.

Another set of questions exist about where the organization should sit in the value chain. Should it manufacture components, should it outsource manufacture, should it become an OEM (original equipment manufacturer), or should it own the distribution channel?

One of the most common mistakes made by organizations (both large and small) attempting to launch a new business is a focus on the first business model idea that occurs to them. There are usually a wide range of business models that can be employed, and there should be a thorough evaluation to determine which is the most valuable, balanced-risk position to hold.

5   Business planning

As with any new venture, it is essential that the vision, rationale, intended activities and milestones are captured and presented in a clear and concise plan. Many corporates fail at this stage because they fail to treat the business as a new venture, rather than just another product. This means the plan needs to address not just the IP, the application and the financials, but also:

■ Long-term sustainability – where is the future pipeline of products going to emerge from beyond the initial IP application?

■ Organizational structure – how best should the business be organized to gain advantage from the size and agility of a start-up, while at the same time, build on the competitive advantages that the parent brings?

■ Incentivization – start-ups are inherently more risky places to work than large companies, yet the rewards for success can be much greater. How will this be recognized in the employment terms of staff?

■ Operations and systems – should the new venture take advantage of assets operated by the parent (call centres, IT systems, HR departments, marketing and communications)? Will integration increase the time to market and restrict operational flexibility?

Above all, the corporate parent needs to be clear about its intention to ultimately exit the venture or not. This will have an impact on all of the above questions. For example, equity stakes for staff will only be valuable if the business is eventually sold or floated.

6   Implementation

Research undertaken by Edengene reveals that, while many companies believe they have plenty of new ideas or surplus IP, less than 20 per cent feel they have the full range of skills necessary to build new businesses. Experience shows that implementation often fails in two key areas. The first is management. It is generally preferable to have some of the originators of the IP move into senior roles in the new venture. This does not, however, make them chief executives overnight! Careful consideration needs to be given at the outset to the make-up of the management team. It may be necessary to bring in senior managers from the outside with a track record of building start-ups in the target market. Venture capitalists place as much emphasis on the quality of a management team as they do on the business idea: corporate venturers should do the same.

The second is business development. Winning customers, establishing key partnerships and perhaps even pulling off a smart acquisition or two are key ingredients of entrepreneurial success. Unfortunately, large companies often struggle to operate with the necessary agility required to deliver these at speed.

Key milestones for this part of commercial development are just as important as technical targets, and can help to manage the venture performance. Failure to meet commercial milestones might indicate that the team needs reinforcing, or that the business proposition is less compelling than originally thought.

Conclusion

Corporate venturing is now an established tool for managing and realizing value from legacy IP. However, many corporates find it difficult to create valuable new ventures, partly because of a lack of innovation and partly because of the difficulty of creating the necessary entrepreneurial culture. Nevertheless, technology advances have made mining a legacy IP portfolio easier than ever before, and as a consequence the likelihood of finding some real gems in the portfolio is substantially increased.

A structured approach to corporate venturing, and a clear understanding of the objectives at the outset, can eliminate a number of the common problems, but the biggest challenge is to think like entrepreneurs, not like corporate managers.

The potential value of corporate venturing can be huge: if Nokia had 'stuck to their knitting' it would still be a wood pulp business, not a mobile communications giant; Disney would be a film company, not a global entertainment giant. If Dixons had not invested £1 million in Freeserve it would not have realized the £1 billion valuation on exit; and if Securicor had not exploited its mobile communications expertise, there would not be an mmO_2.

Julian Wheatland is Director of Corporate Development and a founder of Edengene, the leading growth and corporate venturing business. (His contribution is © Edengene Limited 2004.) Julian is a recognized and regularly quoted expert in corporate venture finance, with wide experience of structuring and financing new business ventures. He is a Chartered Engineer and specializes in the financing and development of early stage intellectual property and technology. For further details contact: julian.wheatland@edengene.com

Collaborative research and development

A relationship to share knowledge and experience can get messy, warns Alan Fiddes at Urquhart-Dykes & Lord, unless you work out how the relationship is going to work in advance.

Bringing together sets of knowledge and experience to develop and exploit new ideas can have substantial benefits for the parties involved. However, as with any relationship there can be problems. Most of them can be avoided or minimized with a little planning and thought at the start of the process, but they can be extremely damaging and expensive if things go wrong later on. The purpose of this article is not so much to answer the questions but to provoke some thought into what questions should be asked in the first place.

Have an agreement

While this might seem obvious it is surprising how many companies and individuals are prepared to start a working relationship with another organization without actually understanding the nature of the relationship between the parties, their respective obligations and rights, and what happens at the end of the agreement. While it is easy to form a relationship while everyone is working in the spirit of cooperation, it is surprising that what seemed to be agreed and understood by both sides at the start of an agreement is the basis of a dispute when things go wrong. As a rule it is always worth taking the next step of transferring what is agreed, or more importantly what each party thinks he or she has agreed when the parties shake hands on a deal, to an agreement in writing, even if it is a simple exchange of e-mails that sets out the basis on which the parties are going to collaborate.

What the agreement should contain

In an article of this length it is not possible to give a detailed description of all the terms that this type of agreement should or can contain. However, this article aims to highlight some of the key issues that should be considered from an intellectual property (IP) perspective.

Ownership

Who will own the rights to the results of the collaboration? Is the agreement that one party will simply carry out research for the other, which will then pay for that work, or will both parties jointly own the rights to the results? If both parties will own the rights, how will those rights be divided? Will they own the resulting rights equally, or will each party have the rights to exploit the results in respect of a particular area of technology, or alternatively the right to exploit the results in a specific geographical area? Once the question of ownership is determined, it is possible to look into issues such as how the rights that are created by one party will need to be transferred to the other party, or how they will be jointly held. For example, do the parties need to establish a separate company to hold the rights and the obligations on each party to protect any property rights that have been created?

Protection

As with any research and development process the result will usually lead to the creation of a number of legal rights. Some of these will arise automatically, such as copyright in drawings, reports and computer programs, while others will need to be registered, such as patents, designs and trade marks. As some of these rights can be lost through prior disclosure, the questions that arise are who is responsible for protecting these rights, for ensuring they are correctly transferred from the inventor, developer or artist to the proper party, and often most importantly, who is responsible for the incurred costs.

In addition to securing the rights, consideration should be given to what happens if those rights are infringed. Who will make the decisions about who will take action against an alleged infringer, what will be the obligations on either party to cooperate in such an action, and again, who will bear the costs of defending the IP rights that have been created as a result of the collaborative research and development? In addition, if an action is successful, how will any damages be divided, or if it is lost, how will the costs be apportioned? Consideration should also be given to what happens if the results of the agreement infringe the rights of a third party. Again, who is responsible for defending alleged infringement action against one or other of the parties? Who will make the decision how the action is dealt with, and who will bear the costs of any proceedings or the award of any damages made against the parties? Will either party indemnify the other against any claim made against it as a result of the other party's use of the results of the research?

In some cases where the R&D results in products being put on the market, consideration may need to be given to responsibility for such matters as statutory obligations for testing, obtaining clearance for relevant authorities, and the question of what happens if there is a product liability claim made against one or other party as a result of a consumer being injured by a product.

Confidentiality

This raises two key issues. The first is the treatment of confidential information that the parties to the agreement exchange, and the second is the treatment of the results of the research. As with any exchange of confidential information, the key is to identify the information that is confidential, and to ensure that its confidential nature is brought to the attention of the party to which it is disclosed. At the start it is clearly advisable to define who can see the confidential information and what uses it can be put to, and ensure that these requirements are complied with. The second issue is how the results of the R&D project will be treated. Consideration should be given to what happens to the results, and what uses either party can make of them outside the terms of the agreement. Clearly if there are obligations of confidentiality it would not be possible to use the results to develop further products for third parties if that involved disclosing the confidential information to them.

Exploitation

Once the R&D has been completed, what happens next? If one party is simply providing R&D services and the results are the property of the other party, the issue is clear-cut, or so one might think. However, even in this straightforward scenario things might not be so simple. For example, can the researcher use the results as a basis for further research for either him- or herself or a third party? Can the researcher take the results and apply them to another technological area? Can the researcher use parts of, for example, a copyright work such as a computer program to create new works for third parties? Even if the parties agree to share the results of the research, there should be some clarity as to how the results can be exploited and how the benefits will be shared.

If the parties are going to agree to divide up the geographical areas in which the R&D can be exploited, there might in certain instances be issues of competition law that need to be taken into consideration: for example, if the agreement relates to the free movement of goods within the European Union.

Termination (or what happens when it all goes terribly wrong)

The one thing that many companies do not think about, especially when entering into a new collaborative agreement, is what happens if it does not work. However, this is the basis of many of the disputes arising from this type of relationship. If the agreement comes to an end because either a project has been completed or the parties are unable to work together, it is important to have some idea of what happens next and what are the continuing obligations on each party in the future. At the most basic level consideration should be given to what happens to the physical embodiment of the research, who is responsible for keeping and storing the results and any associated material, and how long that obligation is to continue. Another issue is, of course, the continuing obligation of confidentiality that might be imposed on either party as a result of the agreement. Clearly, if one party has given confidential information to the other party, then just because the agreement has come to an end it does not mean that the duties of confidentiality end. In addition, if the project itself has resulted in the development of confidential information, there is a continuing obligation on both parties to maintain the confidentiality in that material.

If the agreement has come to an end as a result of a dispute, the parties should think about how that dispute can be settled. Clearly litigation is expensive and time-consuming, and there are alternatives that might be better for the parties: for example, alternative dispute resolution, mediation and arbitration. Whichever route is chosen, the process for settling a dispute should be clear-cut and the parties should agree that they will abide by the decision-making process they have chosen. Again, issues such as the jurisdiction of courts or the selection of an arbitrator should be considered before the dispute breaks out.

Conclusion

We hope this article has been thought-provoking, so that these types of issues can be dealt with at the beginning of an agreement rather than when parties are in dispute or are simply unsure of what was agreed in the first place. The simple step of actually writing down and agreeing what each party thinks it has agreed to is a sensible commercial step, and will often lead to avoiding disputes or at least avoiding expensive litigation in the future.

For further information contact: Alan Fiddes, Urquhart-Dykes & Lord, Tower House, Merrion Way, Leeds, LS2 8PA, GB; tel: +44 113 245 2388; fax: +44 113 243 0446

Buying and selling companies

Identify and settle any IP issues before settling on a price for any acquisitions or disposals, says Antony Rumboll at Bristows.

Every company owns or uses intellectual property (IP). However, with advances in technology, a company's IP might in many cases relate to (or even be the foundation of) its core business. Whether a company intends to purchase the shares of another company (the 'target'), or simply some of its assets (including its IP), the approach that must be taken to identifying the target's IP is essentially the same. For the purposes of this article we assume there is to be a share purchase, so we also consider how a buyer can protect itself against prior use of the target's IP. The approach can be split into three categories:

1. Identifying the IP itself; termed the 'due diligence' process.
2. If relevant, agreeing whether certain IP should be assigned or licensed.
3. Agreeing what protection the buyer can gain from the seller including, for instance, how the seller can lessen its exposure against prior use.

Due diligence

Under English law the rule of *caveat emptor*, or buyer beware, applies. A buyer must therefore carry out its own investigation of the IP owned, or used, by the target in order to identify any issues relating to that IP, including:

- Is it buying the IP necessary for the target to carry out its business and/or for any other intended purpose?
- Is the IP subject to any validity or infringement claims?
- Are the registered IP rights about to expire?
- Can the buyer take the benefit of any IP licences or is there a 'change of control' provision under which the licence will terminate?
- What is to happen to IP that is owned by the target but used by other companies in the target's current group (sometimes called 'shared IP')? Will this shared IP be assigned to the buyer, and then a licence granted back to the seller, or will it be retained by the seller, and a licence granted to the buyer?

These and many other issues will need to be resolved by the buyer, and a negotiation of the price may result! Consequently, a typical due diligence checklist is as follows:

- What is the registered IP owned by the target and used in its business? Is it still registered and when does it expire?
- What is the principal unregistered IP owned and used by the target? Are there any rights that could be registered?
- Have IP licences been granted to any third parties?
- Is there any IP used in the company's business not owned by the seller or target company but used under a licence?
- Are there arrangements for the disclosure of confidentiality agreements in place?
- Are there any challenges or disputes relating to, for example, the validity, of any of the target's IP?
- Are there or have there been any infringements of the target's IP? Has the target infringed anyone else's IP?

Assignments or licences of IP

The buyer may also need to negotiate assignment(s) and/or licence(s) of certain IP. This is usually for two reasons: first, the current contractual arrangements under which that IP is used or exploited from a third party will not remain in place following the acquisition – for instance, there is a change of control provision and under which it terminates – and/or second, the buyer requires the current arrangements to be formalized or strengthened.

In order to identify if IP rights are to be assigned or licensed, it is useful to identify whether rights are used exclusively by the target. If a target company uses its IP exclusively, it will be right that the IP be assigned to the buyer. However, if the IP is also used by, for example, other companies in a group of companies (that is, it is shared IP), it might be right that the IP be only licensed to the buyer.

Contractual protections: warranties, disclosure and indemnities

When shares are acquired, the buyer acquires all liabilities of the target (including all historical liabilities, for example for past infringements). It is vital, therefore, that a buyer seeks contractual protections from the seller by way of warranties and, if relevant, indemnities. Please note that usually, limitations on the seller's liability for warranty claims are agreed. For example, liability might be capped to the purchase price and limited to a certain period after completion.

Warranties are statements of fact verified by the seller and achieve two purposes. The first is to bring to the attention of the buyer any points that are likely to be of concern. Second, they impose a liability on the seller and provide the buyer with a remedy if the statement turns out to be false, and as a consequence the value of the target is reduced. In effect, they allocate risk between the buyer and seller.

A buyer will always seek IP warranties from the seller to ensure that it fully understands the extent and strength of the IP portfolio, and also to protect against any potential liabilities that have been or might be incurred by the target. Clearly, the extent and nature of the warranties differs on every transaction, and will need to be 'tailored' to the type of IP used or owned by the target. The most common warranties are that:

- the target owns the IP it is purporting to sell;
- all IP registrations are subsisting and all renewal fees have been paid;
- the IP owned by the target, or licensed in by the target, is all that is required or desirable;
- the target's IP is free from any third-party rights;
- the target is able to dispose of its IP;
- there are no claims against the target or the sellers relating to the target's IP;
- the target has not infringed the IP of a third party.

If, as is likely, certain of the warranties prove to be untrue, the seller is entitled to disclose against them, specifying the basis on which they are not true. If it does so 'fairly' it will not be liable for such breach in the future. If this disclosure exercise and/or due diligence reveals problems concerning the target's IP, the buyer is typically faced with two choices (assuming the problem is not so fundamental that the buyer does not wish to proceed): to seek a reduction in the purchase price to take account of the liability, or if the problem is only a potential liability, to seek an indemnity, or a 'contractual right' to be reimbursed from the seller. This will provide the buyer with full compensation for any loss suffered. The buyer just needs to ensure that the indemnity is given by a person or company of substance.

Practical steps

In conclusion, there are two practical tips for readers. First, ensure that you or your company has an IP portfolio that adequately protects the company and allows it to carry on its business – either by protecting its own IP or by ensuring that it has all necessary IP licences for it to carry on its business. Second, ensure that a proper record management policy is in place so that information is accessible. All files (relating to both registered and unregistered IP) should be up to date and complete. This will not only make the process easier but might ensure you get the appropriate value for the company!

Antony Rumboll is an Associate at Bristows, a leading intellectual property law firm. He has a scientific background and works in the corporate department. Prior to this he worked for two years in Bristows' intellectual property department. Antony now specializes in all aspects of corporate law and has experience of a wide variety of corporate and commercial matters, including mergers and acquisitions, private equity financings and IPO's.

Bristows is a law firm dedicated to serving businesses with interests in intellectual property and technology, in various industry sectors. The firm has an international reputation in this area and has developed one of the largest IP practices in Europe. Bristows' niche strength mean that the firm is well placed to provide legal advice to growing and new companies. The majority of the firm's lawyers first trained as scientists or engineers. This gives Bristows an unparalleled understanding of, and enthusiasm for, its clients' core businesses.

Prentice & Matthews
PATENT AND TRADE MARK ATTORNEYS

Calvert's Buildings, 52B Borough High Street, London SE1 1XN

Tel: +44 (0)20 7403 8565   Fax: +44 (0)20 7403 8566

E-mail: info@prenmatt.co.uk   Web site: www.prenmatt.co.uk

Your intellectual property may well be your company's greatest asset. For advice and protection of that vital asset, in the UK and around the world, contact us.

Patents

If you or your company invents something, then you want to benefit from that creativity. A patent gives you the right to prevent others from copying your invention for 20 years. If anybody infringes your patent you may take legal action and seek damages. Prentice & Matthews have over 40 years experience, particularly in the fields of transport (automotive, aeronautical and marine) and engineering.

Warning: Do not disclose your idea to anyone until you have been advised by a suitably qualified Patent Attorney. Premature disclosure may prejudice your right to a valid patent.

Trade Marks

Trade Marks protect the various means of identification by which goods or services are distinguished from other traders. Trade Marks are used to identify a particular brand or manufacturer and thereby provide protection for the goodwill and reputation a company has established in its goods and services. Trade Marks can be any sign or combination of signs, words, symbols or logos.

Choosing a good trade mark at an early stage is vital. Many trade marks adopted are unregistrable or conflict with prior registrations. You should not use a trade mark without first asking us to effect a search for prior rights. The registration process is complex and sound advice can save time and, more importantly, cost.

IF YOU USE A TRADE MARK – REGISTER IT!
IF YOU REGISTER A TRADE MARK – USE IT!

Designs

In the UK designs may be protected either by registered design or unregistered design right.

Registered design protection is for the "eye appeal" of the new design (the registration can be invalidated by showing that the design is not new) and subject to the payment of renewal fees will last 25 years.

Unregistered design right arises automatically under English and European Union law in much the same way as copyright. The owner of a design right has the exclusive right to reproduce the design for commercial purposes by making articles to that design or by making a design document recording the design for the purpose of enabling the articles to be made. The right will last for 10 years from the end of the year when the article was first marketed or 15 years after it was first designed – whichever period expires first. For the last 5 years of a design right's life anyone may obtain a licence as of right.

European Patent Attorneys • Chartered Patent Attorneys • Trade Mark Attorneys

R.G.C Jenkins & Co
26 Caxton Street
London SW1H 0RJ
Tel: +44 20 7931 7141
Fax: +44 20 7222 4660
E-mail: info@jenkins-ip.com
Internet: www.jenkins-ip.com

Other offices:
209 Franziskanerhof,
Franziskanerstrasse 16,
D-81669 München,
Germany

Edificio Marina
Avda Maisonnave 41-6C
03003 Alicante
Spain

Contact patent partners: M. Baldwin, K.R. Brown, S.D. Burke, J.P.A. Cross,
H.C. Dunlop, R.E. Jacob, D.C. Musker, T.G. Pendered,
F. Rummler, H.E.A. Whitlock

Contact trade mark partners: H.M. Buckley, R.D. George, S.R. James, J.M.C. John,
T.G. Pendered

Contact design partners: D.C. Musker, T.G. Pendered or any of the above

Areas of specialisation:

We specialise in all areas of intellectual property protection on a worldwide basis. We advise on all aspects of patents, know how, trade marks, domain names, designs and design copyright. Amongst the services we offer are search facilities to clear inventions, trade marks and designs for registration and use around the world, the filing of applications in the UK, Europe and elsewhere, the prosecution of those applications to grant and the enforcement of those registered rights against infringers. We also advise on the licensing of IP rights to third parties and the management and overall strategic development of our clients' intellectual property portfolios.

Our patent attorneys offer expertise in the fields of electronics, including telecommunications and other IT related areas, biotechnology and other life sciences, chemistry, including pharmaceuticals, and mechanical engineering. In addition, our trade mark attorneys handle all aspects of trade mark work, including advice on unfair competition and domain names, whilst our design team deals with the protection of registered and unregistered designs, both at the national and the Community level.

Our IP experts are ably supported by a team of experienced records staff who closely monitor the progress of all IP rights under our care, as well as an IT group who ensure that the firm is at the forefront of technology in our practice as well as our knowledge.

4

Issues by sector

Manufacturing

Stephen Morris, IP Manager at Ricardo plc, which undertakes research, design, development and strategic services for the world's automotive manufacturers, always bears four points in mind in managing its portfolio.

Ricardo can trace its association with intellectual property (IP) to 1906 and holds records detailing IP management back to 1913. The management of IP at that time was firmly limited to patents, where management consisted of the careful recording and filing in ledgers of such details as patent drafts, first filing details, patent numbers, published and granted patent documents, renewal costs and foreign filing dates. The careful recording of these details is as highly significant now as it was almost 100 years ago, and Ricardo still uses the same patent family designation coding system started in 1913.

The record system now used, however, resides within the internal Internet system, and details these most important basic facts along with other details such as links to the company accounting system, allowing instant details of costs per patent family to be retrieved, an identification of the 'patent champion' responsible for exploitation, and the innovations review process allowing member companies within the group to suggest, control and take ownership in innovations submitted prior to acceptance for patent protection. Importantly, all these details are visible to every employee with secure access to internal systems.

However, IP management today requires the practitioner to cover a much wider remit, and perhaps might be more correctly termed 'successful know-how and innovation; direction, identification, protection and exploitation management', where the success can be gauged in measurable performance targets and the value of the IP protected.

It is obvious that the value of IP can be measured in terms of the income generated by licensing or sale. We should also remember, however, the more intangible value to technology companies in proving technical and innovative credibility among peers.

To revisit the four points detailed above might provide suggestions of what areas a company might find suitable in the management of IP in a commercial engineering environment.

Direction

Within a technology-rich company, research delivers the greatest opportunity to create innovation that is owned and exploitable. Research direction is all-important as reinvention is costly in term of money and time and might, if it goes over old ground, lead to conflict with others' IP rights. A patent review is always a good idea at this early planning stage. One example of research guidance is the use of technology roadmaps. The map details the current position, the technical destination and the required route to achieve this. It is highly possible that the overall enabling innovation will lie in the solution to one of the smaller objectives along the route and not in the final step.

The roadmap can also detail the comparative cost of the route taken, so this can be gauged against the market forces within the industry. For example, an innovation blocking competitors along a high-cost route might be easily circumnavigated by a lower-cost route. Conversely, the innovation controlling the low-cost route that has a higher-cost alternative might provide an gauge to the value that could be realized from the licence or sale of the innovation.

Haphazard IP generation can be somewhat of a double-edged sword in that it is unlikely to be closely allied to directed research, and might not be within a core competence of the company. Here it is obviously important to verify ownership of such IP. However, haphazard IP must be considered somewhat sceptically, especially if it is non-core and does not have an obvious exploitation route or in-house expertise to assist in exploitation.

Identification

Internal awareness of patents and innovations has been important as this provides an everyday reminder to all of IP issues, award schemes, recent inventions and so on. A simple display board in prominent places is a must, as are regular updates and lectures on IP.

Engineers and technologists are inherently enthusiastic when problems are solved, and are often only too happy to find someone with whom they can discuss the innovation and solutions. It is important to provide education so that the individual can initially identify inventiveness. Only too often an engineer or technologist applies many years of know-how to a solution, only to consider the result not inventive because of the perceived simplicity with which the solution was arrived at. Providing IP education to technical staff and an in-house route for innovation screening, with a reward structure, has potential to significantly increase the identification of IP.

Selection of innovation

Significantly, almost all engineering IP protection is reliant on the patent system, secrecy or contract agreements. Copyright is important for reports and software sales but the majority of technology protection rests within the patent system. It is important to review the technology before deciding on the route to protection. It is possible for a scoring system to be appropriate for this, for example rating the following criteria, with perhaps a scaling factor for some criteria that are considered to be of overriding importance in a particular technology. This can provide an objective score to assess if the innovation is appropriate for patent protection.

Is the innovation:

- workable/possible?
- robust?
- economically feasible?
- easy to manufacture?
- of significant benefit?
- relevant to core business?
- novel (search done)?
- exploitable?
- likely to achieve a significant market?
- policeable?

Does the innovation:

- have an obvious application?
- solve a current market problem?
- create a highly commercial opportunity?
- provide academic credibility?

Exploitation

Within the engineering environment exploitation will only be achieved by a very limited number of innovations. In order to have any chance of success an innovation must have a reason for exploitation. This might appear simplistic, but unless a coherent and sensible reason can be found for the use of an innovation it will not be exploitable, no matter how hard it is marketed. It is always important to provide a product demonstrator, coupled with evidence of technical and commercial benefits. These benefits must be tangible to the organization to which innovation is sold. In many cases what is being sold is the potential product and not the patent. The patent is there to provide the inventor with rights that can be exercised in return for a fee or a licence.

It is important for inventors to do their homework and not offer the innovation to any body unless there are reasons that it would make something genuinely better for that body. Often exploitation must be autocratic, with the responsible decision maker being available to make the deal right there and then. If the innovation is being sold or licensed from one organization to another, getting the two CEOs talking is a good start.

Overall exploitation will rely on total commitment to the technology, enthusiasm and drive, coupled with technical credibility and honesty. Inventors also require the ability to respond to in-house technological challenge and the 'not invented here' syndrome they will encounter from many manufacturers they approach.

Stephen Morris is the IP Manager for Ricardo UK Ltd, one of the world's foremost independent automotive consultancies, undertaking research, design, development and strategic services to the world's automotive manufacturers.

IP and the creative industries

IP is the contract law for the creative economy, says John Howkins at ITR. And just like any contract matter, it can be well or badly managed.

It is often said that the creative industries have a special understanding of intellectual property. Their success, even their survival, depends entirely on having new ideas and turning those ideas into money. At all levels from the freelance designer to the company director, they deal in creativity, innovation and invention as a matter of course. It is their individual preoccupation, source of social status and prime source of revenue. They had relied in this way upon their brains for some time – say, a few centuries – before terms like human and intellectual capital became fashionable in business schools and corporate training centres. They practically invented the philosophical principles of intellectual property, and we owe copyright to a group of disgruntled English writers in the early 18th century.

We also owe modern patents to individual inventors about a century later. Although I strongly believe that the scientific research that produces patentable ideas is as creative as any artistic, literary or dramatic activity, I shall use the modern, narrower sense of 'creative industries' which excludes science. From now on I shall focus on the arts and other industries that use copyright.

Copyright is two things. First, it consists of the laws that set out the works that can be protected, and the limitations and exemptions to that

protection. Then there is the licensing process by which rights holders negotiate how they want their rights to be used. These negotiations result in
contracts specifying format, media, territory, language, the time span of a
licence, and so on. IP is the contract law for the creative economy, and, just
like any contract matter, it can be either well or badly managed.

The achievement of the creative industries has been to devise a set of
contractual arrangements that are suited for the use of ideas rather than the
exchange of corn, manufactured goods or services. This sentence immediately needs a qualification. Although the creative industries thrive off ideas,
copyright law is entirely about works, which are expressions of ideas, such
as a book or a piece of music. (It is dogma in the copyright world that one
cannot copyright an idea, one can only copyright its expression.) In practice,
business people care little for works as such and are primarily concerned
with buying and selling rights in the work.

First comes the imagination and collaboration – sometimes a meeting of
minds, sometimes a bloody row – that moves people's ideas along, and thus
moves the business along. The second is the moment when this creative
maelstrom becomes visible, explicit and can be monetized. This occurs
when the idea is given a name and can be defined as a work. At this point, the
person who has the idea owns the work and acquires rights over it.

The aim of copyright exploitation is to salami-slice the work, to create
as many rights as possible, and to find buyers who will pay the largest
amount for each right for the shortest possible time. A fee of £10 for the
right to use a work for one year is 10 times as valuable as a fee of £10 to
use it for 10 years.

Of course, people who lack the inclination, time and skill to license their
own rights will sell out all their rights in one fell swoop. These people are
valuing a bird in the hand over a whole flock in the bush. Others, such as
investors and agents, then take on the role of licensing. The variety and
number of rights in most copyright works (a film, a story, a character) are
theoretically infinite. Even a low-budget British film will bundle together a
few hundred copyrights into one big new work. A big-budget US movie will
have over a thousand rights. This is on the input side. On the sales side, the
way in which these rights are then licensed is infinite. The skill is in
wielding the salami knife in the most efficient and rewarding manner.

The way to maximize copyright value is to:

- have ideas that can be privatized;
- have ideas that can be privatized by you;
- have ideas that copyright law will accept as defined works;
- have works that can be divided into as many rights as possible;
- know the rights market (that is, do not try to sell film rights in the television market, or haute couture rights on the high street);

∎ strike a balance between the infinite elasticity of intangible rights and the need to find a buyer with as little fuss as possible.

In this way, copyright is an elegant and efficient way of valuing assets and providing a legal basis for negotiating contracts.

People's attitudes to copyright generally fall into three categories. A few people who are driven by their internal creative passions treat copyright as an afterthought. This is inefficient unless they manage a profitable buy-out. The second approach is to seek to copyright everything, but too much copyright can be as dangerous as too little. These people are like bean-counters who think only of money. A third approach steps back from copyright solely as a piece of property, and integrates the creative process and the business model.

It is worth mentioning two misconceptions. The first, hinted at above, is that more copyright is automatically a good thing. In fact, the creative industries' attitude to copyright varies widely, from unquestioned commitment to puzzled uncertainty and even hostility. In the first group are the large corporations whose market dominance depends on selling multiple, identical copies in fields such as film, publishing, television, music and design. In a second group lie artists and advertising, architecture, craft and fashion companies, where attitudes to the ownership of ideas is more ambiguous and where attitudes to IP are consequently more volatile. And in a third small but vocal group lie a group of computer programmers and others who support open source and free software and the new Creative Commons licence. It is important to be aware of these ambiguities because it reminds us of the idiosyncratic nature of creative work and of the real nature of copyright.

The second common misconception is related. It is clear that copyright practices differ widely between industries. The law differs a bit, but licensing practices can differ enormously. The way in which copyright is licensed is totally dependent on the nature of the industry. To take a small example, the terms and conditions of making publicity images available to the media are substantially different in the film and television businesses; and different again in fashion, design and book publishing. Someone who has worked in film distribution or fashion will have acquired an intuitive understanding of how much to pay and what price to charge. People from other industries, asked to negotiate rights in these fields, will flounder.

Managing copyright must start at the centre of the business. Companies should set an IP strategy in the same way as (presumably?) they have a financial strategy. The board should include someone with IP expertise. I despair at companies that depend on IP but which do not have a board member with any IP expertise.

IP should be a profit centre, not a cost centre. The company should run an annual IP audit. If the company is public, it should report on its IP in its annual accounts. Investors need to know how the company is making its assets work for them.

Managers' annual targets and evaluation should include IP. If managers are unaware of IP, they should be offered a training course. Many workers are becoming more aware of their own worth as the creators of ideas. Human resources (HR) departments need to ensure they have reasonable employment contracts, and that management practices allocate IP fairly. I have seen some contracts that would be rejected by the courts for being restrictive or even, in one case, against the Human Rights Act. Sensitivity is needed here.

It is important to remember the basic reason for copyright; by which I mean the reason for having ideas in the first place. Managing copyright is about managing a business, whether in film or retailing, in such a way as to strike the right balance between new ideas and their delivery to the public.

John Howkins is a director of ITR, an international firm advising companies on IP in the media, entertainment, communications and creative sectors. Clients include the London Development Agency, Universal Studios, Time Warner, the Arts Council England, Creative Business School, UNCTAD and IP East. He is author of the *The Creative Economy* (Penguin, 2002). For further information, contact John Howkins on +44 (20) 7434 1400 or john@johnhowkins.com

Consumer goods

Intellectual property and the protection it affords are prerequisites to the existence of brands, says John Noble at the British Brands Group.

In an aggressively competitive world, how do you prevent others from stealing your investment, taking a slice of your action and reaping rewards that should rightfully be yours? This is a fundamental question for senior managers in consumer goods companies. The cynic might view it solely in the context of safeguarding corporate wealth and delivering shareholder value, but that is a small part of the picture. The question strikes at the heart of brand competitiveness.

Branded businesses strive to build and sustain close, meaningful relationships with their individual customers, which are achieved by delivering against a clear, distinct promise consistently over time. Domestos bleach promises to kill germs, Andrex tissue promises to be longer and stronger, an Innocent drink promises to be natural, honest and lovingly made. But in today's market a brand must deliver more than consistent performance. Consumers demand results at ever better value, from companies that behave ethically, responsibly and sustainably.

Brands reside in the minds of individuals, and successful brands are those that an individual knows, trusts and believes in to the extent that he or she will buy that brand over competitors' brands. To earn such 'mindspace' is neither easy nor cheap. It takes years to build, and everything a company says and does plays its part. It is also easily destroyed, by a competitor delivering better performance or value (such as Dell computers' impact on IBM and Compaq) or when a crisis hits (for instance, Perrier water's contamination incident).

However, brand 'mindspace' – or brand equity – once created is enormously valuable. It is the reason people buy a particular product today and tomorrow. It is the source of competitive edge and the basis for future cash flow. This value is well recognized by markets, where branded companies command higher share prices, reflecting their more reliable and predictable future earnings potential. (See Figure 4.3.1.) It is also increasingly recognized by companies themselves, with around 60 per cent of chief executives at the World Economic Forum in Davos in 2004 attributing 40 per cent or more of the market value of their companies to their brands.

If, as we have seen, this value is vulnerable, how can companies protect themselves and their investment from imitators and the unscrupulous who wish to free-ride on the reputation and loyalty that has been created?

Keeping imitators at bay

The threat from imitators is ever-present, and in a world where functional performance can be replicated in a matter of a few months, very real. The competitive response from branded goods companies consists of constant innovation to stay ahead and the building of ever-stronger relationships with consumers.

A strong brand is itself a powerful defence against imitation. An imitator might find it relatively straightforward to replicate the burger, fries and soft

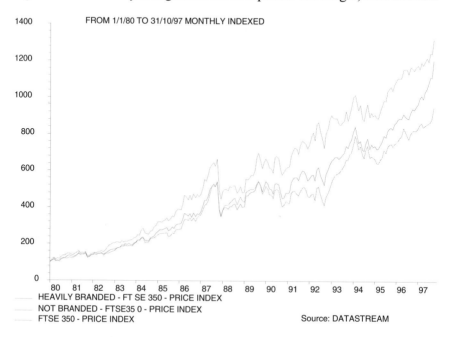

Figure 4.3.1 The share prices of branded and unbranded companies compared
Source: Datastream

drink offer of McDonald's restaurants, but would find it extremely difficult – and expensive – to match the whole of its brand, including its character and reputation.

Intellectual property rights provide a further source of protection, safeguarding the investment and risk involved in bringing new ideas to market. Gillette is one example of a company that seeks such protection. Were it not to do so, its innovations would quickly be replicated, depriving it of the necessary return on investment and destroying its potential competitive edge. IP protection was considered right from the early development stages of its groundbreaking Oral B CrossAction toothbrush, with the protectability of each improvement being carefully considered prior to its incorporation into the product. The aim was to create a 'thorny thicket' of protection around the product, making it as difficult as possible for imitators to get too close. The final product was covered by four design registrations, trade mark rights in the Oral B and CrossAction names, and 23 patents covering inventions from the filaments and the handle to the manufacturing process itself.

Fighting the counterfeiter

The counterfeiter takes imitation to extreme, matching branded products so closely – right down to using the same name and logo – that they are frequently indistinguishable from the originals in appearance. Major criminals control the trade in fakes, using the profits to fund other serious organized crime, including terrorism. Brands are the usual target because their value, reputation and consumer franchise deliver a large market and assured sales. Easy profit, over-stretched enforcement authorities and relatively light penalties if caught, combined with the convenient use of existing criminal networks, make this a very 'soft' crime, which costs the UK economy an estimated £10 billion a year.

The days are past where the counterfeiter concentrated solely on luxury brands such as Chanel, Louis Vuitton and Gucci. Now everyday items are vulnerable, a trend highlighted by Commissioner Bolkestein in his announcement on EU counterfeiting trends in November 2003: 'The latest figures speak volumes: all everyday consumer products are now potential targets for counterfeiting and pirating.' The absence of safety testing for these products, including food, adds a further layer of risk to consumers and their health and well-being.

Action can be taken against counterfeiters in the civil courts by the brand owner, and can result in a criminal prosecution, but without the protection of intellectual property, the fight against counterfeiting would be a lost cause. It is infringement of trade mark rights or copyright that most frequently provides the means to prosecute and impose penalties on the counterfeiter. In the UK the legislative framework is in place to tackle the problem, and

Figure 4.3.2   Persil: one of many products subject to counterfeiting
Source: the Anti-Counterfeiting Group

brand owners would be prudent to use it. However, the limited resources available to enforcement bodies such as trading standards officers, and the low priority sometimes given by the police and local authorities, mean the odds remain stacked in favour of the criminal, and it is often left to the brand owner to take action in the civil courts.

Copycat packaging

The sophistication of the imitator, the limitations of IP protection and the dangers lurking for consumer goods brands are well illustrated by the problem of copycat packaging. Here imitators sail as close to the wind as the law will allow, copying packaging sufficiently closely to mislead consumers but making proving infringement of intellectual property rights extremely difficult.

While the similar packaging might result in some shoppers picking up one product in mistake for the other, it works primarily at a much more sophisticated level. A brand's packaging works as shorthand to the shopper of all the values and past experiences the shopper associates with that brand, a signpost that triggers that brand's 'mindspace'. The shopper picks up these same shorthand, visual cues from the copycat product, mentally associating the brand's qualities with the unknown rival. The effect is subliminal but

Figure 4.3.3 Tesco's 1996 copy of Kellogg's corn flakes

effective, persuading shoppers to switch to the rival without ever being consciously aware of the deception.

A 'thorny thicket' of IP protection around packaging as well as the product provides some – if limited – protection against such attack. However, in the UK at least, this is one area where legislation has yet to catch up with the subtleties of the modern imitator.

IP and branded consumer goods

Intellectual property and the protection it affords are prerequisites to the existence of brands. How can shoppers choose one offer over another unless there are distinctive signposts to allow them to differentiate? How can an organization build trust and reassurance in a product if a competitor, less committed to quality, is free to pass off the organization's goods as its own? Where is the incentive to invest long term in performance and reputation if that investment cannot be protected? How can a company compete if it carries the cost of developing new products, a significant percentage of which will fail in the market, if its competitors copy only the successes and carry none of the development costs?

Bearing in mind that IP rights are so fundamental to the branded business model, it is surprising that the subject does not command greater priority within more companies. Too often it is seen as the preserve of the legal department rather than relevant to the very core of the business. Recent research by Maxima International Consultants found that less than 1 per cent of sales turnover is spent on brand protection, 10 per cent of companies had no brand protection budget at all, and 31 per cent have maintained the same brand protection budget each year (despite evidence from other quarters that brands are becoming increasingly important commercially).

Companies that fail to look to available intellectual property rights and the protection of their brands lay themselves open to attack. They risk lost revenue and increased costs. More seriously, they put their brand equity and their very competitiveness in jeopardy. A copycat attack can hit sales by over 25 per cent. Nestlé was forced to spend £30 million repackaging its coffee range after its previous packaging had been rendered generic through copying. Consumers worry about brand authenticity if they know a particular brand is subject to counterfeiting. More to the point, each pound of revenue lost and additional cost incurred from inadequate brand protection is a pound lost to innovation and brand building. That is a loss to the very heart of brand competitiveness.

The British Brands Group is a membership association of brand manufacturers, committed to building in the UK an environment in which brands may flourish. It works closely with organizations such as the Anti-Counterfeiting Group and the European Brands Association (AIM) in Brussels to ensure that effective legislation and enforcement is in place to encourage investment in innovation and brand building. It has published *A Guide to Brand Protection*, a free guide available to any company keen to protect and preserve its brand. Copies are available by calling 07020 934250, by e-mail to info@britishbrands-group.org.uk or from the Web site www.britishbrandsgroup.org.uk

Financial services and systems

Roberts Franks at Franks & Co discusses the use of patents for business methods and the financial sector.

The area of so-called 'business method' patents is often misunderstood, and like software patents, the subject is of much debate within the patent profession and business community.

There is no generally acceptable definition of a business method invention. However, the US Business Method Improvement Act 2000 defines a 'business method' as being:

a method of (1) (a) administering, managing, or otherwise operating an enterprise or organization, including a technique used in conducting or doing business; or (b) processing financial data; (2) any technique used doing athletics, instruction or personal skills; and (3) any computer-assisted implementation of a method described in paragraph (1) or a technique described in paragraph (2).

It is fair to say that there is a significant difference in approach to the patenting of business inventions between the US Patent Office and patent offices in Europe, including the European Patent Office (EPO). In the United States, there is no doubt that business methods are entitled to patent protection, subject to the usual criteria that the invention is new over prior publications, and is not obvious. However, for inventions that fall within certain classifications of art, primarily concerned with Internet inventions, the US Patent Office will follow a more robust examination procedure, according to the Business Method Improvements Act 2000. Although patent applications for business methods undergo a different examination procedure than that for other patent applications at the US Patent Office, the fundamental criteria for patentability are the same as for any other invention.

In Europe, the position is slightly different, because the European Patent Convention (EPC) contains an exclusion to the patenting of '(a) discoveries, scientific theories and mathematical methods; (b) aesthetic creations; (c) schemes, rules and methods for performing mental acts, playing games or doing business, and programs for computers; (d) presentations of information'. The first potential pitfall is whether the EPO, or national patent office of an individual European country, classifies the invention as being a 'business method invention'. Since there is no widely accepted definition of a business method invention, this process can be inconsistent between different patent applications and different patent offices. In some cases, where different patent applications are prosecuted for related inventions covering the same technology, some of these might be subject to business method invention objections, while other related applications might proceed without any such objection. An example of this is the patent applications for the well-known Amazon 'one click' system, in which some of the patents have progressed to grant without encountering any business method objection, while other patent applications in the suite have been delayed at the EPO by business method objections.

Many patent applications proceed through to grant under the normal process of examination, that is, examination for novelty, inventive step and industrial applicability, without encountering any objection that the invention is the excluded subject matter of a business method per se. On the other hand, if the EPO or national patent office raises a business method objection, the result can be that the patent application is in for a difficult and expensive prosecution. However, for those applicants who persevere through the examination procedure, it is by no means certain that the application will be rejected. Many applications are amended to overcome the objections and proceed through to grant, while retaining a good scope of protection of the underlying invention.

F R A N K S & C O

Chartered Patent Attorneys
European Patent Attorneys

Intellectual Property
Creation and Management

15 Jessops Riverside, Brightside Lane, SHEFFIELD, S9 2RX

Prospect House, 32 Sovereign Street, LEEDS, LS1 4BJ

Compass House, Vision Park, Chivers Way, CAMBRIDGE, CB4 9AD

Imex House, 40 Princess Street, MANCHESTER, M1 6DE

Head Office: +44 (0)114 249 9888

Central Fax: +44 (0)114 249 9666

E-mail (all offices): franksco@franksco.com

Website: http//www.franksco.com

European Patent Office policy

The EPO has repeatedly emphasized the need for any invention to contain a technical contribution in order for a patent to be granted. Much of the EPO case law uses the term 'technical' as if the term was well understood and clearly defined. In fact, there is no definition in the EPC of the concept of technicality, and a recurring problem from case to case is to decide whether a particular invention is of a 'technical' nature or not.

In essence, if an invention can be shown to make a technical contribution to a field of art, then the invention is likely to contain an inventive step – one of the two main criteria for obtaining valid patent protection. What the EPO is looking for in order to grant a claim are technical means for implementing an invention. Claims to an invention completely in the abstract without reference to implementing technology are likely to be rejected as making no technical contribution to the art.

Technical contribution has, in various EPO decided cases, been held to include automation of otherwise manually processed operations. Since a large number of business method inventions include practical apparatus or methods, there are many examples of granted European patents for business method-related inventions.

Business method inventions before the UK Patent Office

The UK Patent Office position is similar to the EPO's. UK Patent Office decisions take into account the body of decided case law under the EPC. However, the UK Patent Office also takes notice of decisions from the UK courts, but it suffers from a basic vacuum of UK case law. Of the cases that have been decided, one in particular stands as a landmark. In Fujitsu's application 1977, the judge stated:

> However, it is and always has been a principle of patent law that mere discoveries or ideas are not patentable, but those discoveries and ideas which have technical aspect or technical contribution are. Thus, the concept that what is needed to make an excluded thing patentable is a technical contribution is not surprising.

According to UK Patent Office practice, inventions that involve a technical contribution will not be refused a patent merely because they relate to a business method. This position brings UK Patent Office practice on business method-related inventions into line with its practice on computer program inventions, and more nearly aligns its practice with that under the corresponding provisions of the EPC.

As with the European procedure, it is important that the specification as originally filed is detailed enough to clearly describe the technical features of the invention, since there is no opportunity to add new subject matter to the patent application after filing.

Which inventions are patentable

Generally, inventions that describe a purely abstract method, divorced of any apparatus or technical means for implementing it, and that could be regarded as 'pure' business methods, will continue to be rejected in Europe. All other classes of invention should be patentable subject to the basic criteria of being new over the state of the art, having an inventive step, and satisfying the criteria for technicality.

The following non-exhaustive list includes types of invention which might be categorized as business method inventions, and for which patents are either pending or have been granted before the EPO or in individual national European states.

▪ Trading systems – includes systems for trading stocks, shares, commodities, derivatives and the like. Examples include:
  - A communication system aimed at overcoming the problems of providing commodities traders with the ability to carry out multiple conversations simultaneously for price sensitive information (GB 2226217 B Reuters Limited).
  - Terminals for effecting trading in fungible properties, such as securities (GB 1489571 B).The system consists of a set of terminals, a data processor, a computer program, recording expressions of interest for buying or selling property and disseminating the expressions of interest to other terminals, entering a bid/offer process and then recording a transaction commanded through a terminal.
  - An automatic world trade exchange system for connecting central exchange computers of commodity exchanges around the world, allowing the exchanges to communicate electronically and allowing users of one exchange to trade with users of another exchange (GB 216521 B).
▪ Electronic fraud detection systems. An example is a fraud detection system based upon artificial intelligence techniques or predictive modelling techniques, for identifying unusual trading patterns on a user account (EP 0669032 B, HNC Inc.)
▪ Systems for storing maps and serving them over the Internet or another communications network, as 'online maps', for example EP 0845124 B.
▪ Gaming systems, particularly where these are computerized. An example is EP 0625760 B for an interactive computerized gaming system with

remote terminals, in which a host computer is programmed to store accounts for players playing a game, and a client terminal simulates playing a casino game.

■ Online brokerage – in which an intermediary acts as a matchmaker for buying and selling parties. Income can be derived by charging fees to buying and/or selling parties.

■ Online shops – examples are extremely prolific on the Internet and typically show a list of goods with descriptive pictures, together with a price and a shopping basket facility. A famous example is Amazon.com.

■ Transformation agents – that is, intermediaries who gather, collate and process data, then sell it on to other users. An example is a supermarket reward point scheme which collects information on consumer shopping habits.

■ Stock market analysis/trading systems – including chart-based systems, neural network or other artificial intelligence systems, Monte Carlo simulations and arbitrage programs.

■ Financial product tools – including loan calculation software and tax calculation software.

■ E-services or online services – these are where a service provider sells an online service, for example download of photographs delivered as data to a user's personal computer, downloads of company reports or the like, and usually characterized by delivery of data rather than delivery of goods.

■ Paper-based systems – systems of physical and/or electronic forms to enable easier collection of data, for example tax return forms, or printing systems to customize the printing of credit card bills to include advertisements or information that is specific to a customer's interest.

■ Billing systems – including paper-based or software-based time recorded and invoice calculation systems, for all firms, automatic telephone charging systems for calculation of a user's bill, and similarly for other utilities such as electricity, gas and water.

■ Business meeting systems – for example hotel reservation systems, meeting room booking systems, and systems for reserving travel facilities.

■ Online distribution systems – including methods of delivering print items ordered over the Internet, for example systems for allocating print jobs to print service providers, in a manner that efficiently utilizes printer resources (GB 2371392 B, Hewlett Packard).

Conclusion

The area of business method patents is a developing area of law, and it is possible that different advisors will give different interpretations of the law, with more or less optimism about the chances of obtaining patent protection for any particular invention. In practice, business methods are seldom implemented in isolation, but require some physical means for their implementation. Items that are not business methods themselves, but that are designed to implement a business method, might form the basis for patentable subject matter.

Managers of patent portfolios need to take a robust commercial view of this area and decide on a cost–benefit basis whether it is worthwhile applying for patent protection for business method-related inventions. Certainly, as far as the US Patent Office is concerned, there is no particular reason to treat a business method or business method-related invention any differently from an invention for any other type of technology. In Europe, there are complications.

Even after taking specific advice, an organization might still be unclear whether to apply for patent protection. However, managers who decide not to apply for patent protection for their business method-related inventions should not be surprised if they find later on that their competitors have obtained granted patents for a similar or the same invention. Managers who fail to protect their inventions in this field risk losing out to competitors.

Robert Franks is a Chartered Patent Attorney and European Patent Attorney with Franks & Co in Sheffield, UK. He is a member of the Computer Technology Committee of the Chartered Institute of Patent Agents, and has specialized in the patenting of software inventions and business method inventions for large multinational clients, and technology start-ups for the past 15 years.

Franks & Co is a full-service intellectual property firm with its head office in Sheffield and offices throughout the UK, dealing with mainly UK, US and multinational corporate clients. For further information contact Robert B Franks, Franks & Co, 15 Jessops Riverside, Brightside Lane, Sheffield S9 2RX; tel: +44(0)114 249 9888; www.franksco.com.

Software

Copyright or patent? Hugh Dunlop at R G C Jenkins & Co discusses protection for software.

Copyright

'Isn't copyright enough to protect a computer program?' is a question many software developers ask. Copyright is critical to the protection of software. It is an inherent right of exclusivity in a work of authorship such as a software program: that is, it is a right that the author (or the person commissioning the work) enjoys without having to register it. Copyright protects the expression of ideas implemented in software, but as we shall see below, it does not protect the ideas themselves.

Copyright protects the skill and labour involved in writing or producing program code, whether high-level code, assembly language or machine code, and is infringed when any substantial part of the code is copied, including copying by transcription between different levels or languages. For infringement of copyright to be proven, there must be actual copying of the protected work, which at the minimum means that the alleged infringer must have had access to the original.

Copyright is, of course, a powerful tool in software licensing. Protecting the working time invested in software is important, but often is not enough. Copyright does not offer any protection against a competitor who arrives at the same idea by an independent route. In cases of particularly valuable code it is not uncommon for a competitor to establish a 'clean room' for development of functionally equivalent code without copying the original code.

By such efforts, the valuable ideas implemented in a software program can be reproduced with impunity if copyright is the only protection. If the ideas underlying the software can be implemented afresh in different code or a different language, a broader form of protection is needed.

Patents

Like other inventions, ideas implemented in software can be protected by patents (subject to certain exclusions below) for up to 20 years (plus as much as one additional year in cases where there is a claim to priority from an earlier patent application), provided they satisfy the usual requirements of novelty and inventiveness. Patent protection has the important advantage over copyright protection in that a patent 'monopoly' is absolute in nature: the patent is infringed when a later developed product or process falls within the scope of its claims, even if the later product or process has been developed independently and without knowledge of the patented invention. Ignorance of the patent is not an excuse for infringement. Thus, patents provide vital protection for ideas implemented in software just as they do for mechanical inventions and new chemicals, processes and the like. Indeed, in many electronic devices the traditional distinction between hardware and software has all but disappeared, and a new and inventive program can frequently be implemented in either hardware or software at the designer's choice.

'But I have heard that software is not patentable'

There is an exclusion in patent law that says a program for a computer as such shall not be regarded as an invention for patent purposes (Patents Act 1977, Section 1(2)(c) and European Patent Convention Article 52(2)), and this gives rise to much confusion and some controversy over what is and is not patentable in this field. US patent law is much more clear in this respect. The US Supreme Court has adopted an all-embracing mantra that 'anything under the sun invented by man' can be patented (*Diamond v Diehr* 450 US 188, referring to the US Congress Committee report of 1952). As a result, patents are allowable in the United States for such matters as new methods of doing business (whether involving a computer or otherwise), new methods of playing a game and so on.

In the UK and Europe, a distinction is drawn between inventions that are 'technical' (and which can be patented) and those that are not. It is beyond the scope of this handbook to explain this difference at length, and readers are advised to explore the texts listed at the end of the chapter or to seek professional advice if a particular invention might be on this borderline. For present purposes, it is important to note that if the problem sought to be

Table 4.5.1 Patentable and non-patentable computer and machine-implemented inventions

	Patentable	Not patentable
Mathematical method	Method of image processing which uses a mathematical method to operate on numbers representing an image (T208/84 *Vicom*). Method of controlling a physical process by application of a mathematical method (T953/94 *Georges*).	Method of digitally filtering data performed on a conventional general purpose computer (T208/84 *Vicom* – Summary of Facts and Submissions Section V).
Method for performing a mental act	Method of manufacture of a computer chip (T453/91 *IBM*).	Method of designing a computer chip (T453/91 IBM). Computer programmed to model a synthetic crystal structure – *Fujitsu's application* [1996] RPC 511 [1997] RPC 608 (CA).
Method for playing a game	A gaming machine characterized by ranked value winning characters (T60/98 *Sigma**).	A method of solving crossword puzzles or a game as an abstract entity defined by its rules (*EPO Guidelines* Chapter IV section 2.3.5).
Method for doing business	Web-enabled system and method for designing a laser scanner, computing a price quotation and sending the quotation to a prospective user (*Metrologic* Patent no. GB2341251*). Automated Securities Trading Apparatus (Merrill Lynch's Patent No GB2180380).	Web-based online user interface permitting a user to specify computer equipment and place an order (*Dell's applications* O/432/01, O/177/02 & O/377/02). Data processing system for making a trading market in securities (*Merrill Lynch's application* [1989] RPC 561 (CA)).*
Program for a computer	Method and system in a data processing system windowing environment for displaying previously obscured information (T935/97 *IBM*).	Read-only memory providing means to evaluate square root of number by improved method (*Gale's application* [1991] RPC 304).
Presentations of information	Display of only valid commands in a computer 'help' system (T887/92 *IBM*).	Gaming machine in which fruit pictures are replaced by advertisements (*Shahin's application* O/149/95).

* Representatives – R G C Jenkins

solved by the invention is not a technical problem but lies in the field of business or administration, or the presentation of information, or performing a mental act (such as designing a building or writing computer code) or playing a game, the solution to the problem through a computer program is unlikely to be considered a patentable invention.

For brevity, and by way of mere example, Table 4.5.1 sets out some computer or machine-implemented inventions that have so far been, or are likely to be, considered patentable or unpatentable. Examples have been selected from among UK Patent Office decisions and EPO decisions, because these are different parallel routes by which an invention may be protected in the UK. The examples are set out with a separate row for each of the relevant exclusions under Section 1(2)(c). An idea implemented in software might fail the test for technicality under any one of these headings.

In the table, 'O' numbered decisions are decisions of the UK Patent Office, and 'T' numbered decisions are decisions of the Technical Boards of Appeal of the EPO. Whereas the UK and European Patent Offices strive to achieve the same standard of patentability for computer-implemented inventions, it must be borne in mind that the legal precedents that apply to the two offices are different, so that on occasion an invention might be viewed more favourably by one office than the other. It must also be borne in mind that the law is continuously developing, and decisions of the patent offices may be overturned by the courts.

Protecting IP in software

Tips for preparing patent applications for computer-implemented inventions

Critical to any patent application is a comprehensive description of the invention, including a workable embodiment. In the case of computer-implemented inventions, this means describing not merely what the software does, but how it does it. This does not, however, mean that a complete program listing is necessary. Computer programs extending over many pages are costly to print and will be laid open for public inspection, but may be omitted from the printed patent application at the discretion of the Patent Office.

Applicants tend not to submit lengthy program listings, but find that program flow diagrams and state diagrams are more convenient ways of describing inventive principles. Also, portions of pseudocode are useful, as they are usually meaningful to patent examiners and can be generalized without obfuscating information that needs to be conveyed. A degree of detail is important in this field, because it is often difficult to predict what prior art will be cited by the Patent Office, and it is useful to have detailed explanations and definitions of terms to fall back on during prosecution of an application, especially if there is the possibility of an objection under Section 1(2)(c) of the Patents Act (or Article 52(2) of the European Patent Convention).

Tips for enhanced copyright protection

There are some basic do's and don'ts for protection of copyright, which need not involve expense but require good housekeeping:

- Keep the original work on a robust medium (for example on a CD ROM) marked with the date of creation, preferably signed by the author. Keep it in a safe place – its value lasts a very long time.
- Ensure that the copyright is assigned in writing from its author to the person or company that commissions it. Both the author and the assignee must sign the assignment. An agreement to assign (such as an agreement commissioning the work) is not enough.
- Mark the original work and all copies with a copyright notice. A typical copyright notice reads '© XYZ Company Ltd 2004. All rights reserved.'
- Consider embedding redundant code and/or deliberate errors which can be probed and identified to prove the code has been copied and not merely developed independently.

Trade secrets and confidentiality

A separate section of a later chapter of this handbook discusses the subject of trade secrets and confidentiality. These rights are as important to software as to other materials.

Trade secrets are like ice. If you put them in the wrong place they will melt away. In the case of software, that process can be as rapid as the Internet itself. Software developers like to work by reviewing (and all too frequently by copying and pasting) the code of others. Once lost, a secret cannot be recaptured, so software companies need to apply particular care to safeguard trade secrets and know-how.

One common distinction is drawn between source code (that is, high-level code meaningful to a software engineer) and object code (machine-level code that can only be understood by a computer). The former is guarded jealously, while the latter is necessarily distributed under licence. Steps might be available to prevent or hinder the decompiling of object code back into source code. Common steps that are taken to protect source code include:

- placing it in escrow under strict terms of release, in preference to making it available to a customer;

- publishing application programmer interface (API) commands so that customers can interface with the code without having to see it;
- careful selection of software consultants who can be permitted access to source code to service the needs of customers, with appropriate contractual restrictions.

Databases

In the UK, there is no quantum level of creativity that needs to be proven for a work to benefit from copyright protection. Mere compilations of data that result from an author's skill and labour enjoy copyright protection. Thus, copyright protection is available for the contents of a database. This is not the case in every country in Europe, and some (such as Denmark) have enacted *sui generis* database protection laws to fill this gap. The above comments for enhanced copyright protection apply to databases, except that a database is typically a work of authorship that grows or evolves over time. Periodically (for instance yearly), a copy should be archived for evidentiary purposes in the event of a dispute over copyright infringement.

Further reading

The following texts expand on the issue of patentability of computer-implemented inventions.

UK Patent Office *Manual of Patent Practice*, Part 1 ss 1–6, especially s 1(2), available at http://www.patent.gov.uk/patent/reference/mpp/ss1–6.pdf
Guidelines for Examination in the European Patent Office, Part C Chapter IV – Patentability, available at http://www.european-patent-office.org/legal/gui_lines/pdf_2003/rlecv75.pdf
CIPA Guide to the Patents Act 5th edn, pp 12–29. ISBN 0 421 650109.

Hugh Dunlop is a partner at R G C Jenkins & Co., Patent and Trade Mark Attorneys in London, where he specializes in communications, electronics and software patents. (This chapter is copyright R G C Jenkins & Co 2004. All rights reserved.) Further information available from R G C Jenkins & Co, 26 Caxton Street, London SW1H 0RJ; Web site: www.jenkins-ip.com

Biotechnology

Biotechnology as a science has emerged in the years since patent laws were originally formulated, says Reuben Jacob at RGC Jenkins & Co.

Why IPRs are important to biotechnology companies

It is widely recognized that intellectual property rights (IPRs) are of particular and often fundamental importance to biotechnology companies, whose ideas might often be their only assets. Therefore a commercially realistic and structured approach to the acquisition and exploitation of these rights, with professional advice at an early stage, is crucial and can be a key to obtaining funding, investment and eventually commercial success.

Biotechnology and patent law

As patents are probably the most important form of intellectual property right for biotechnology companies, this is the main topic that will be dealt with here. The general principles of patent law set out elsewhere in this book apply to biotechnological inventions just as to any other area of technology. But biotechnology as a science has emerged in the years since patent laws were originally formulated. To accommodate this new science, some existing principles of the law have required development, and new principles have had to be formulated. The forces that have driven these processes of development and formulation, such as public policy, considerations of morality and of course the needs of industry, have often been in conflict. This has led to the development of what is perhaps the most detailed and specific set of patent provisions for any technology, embodied in Europe in EU Directive 98/44, and now adopted into the European Patent Convention. Whether these provisions will prove to be a help or a hindrance to the biotechnology industry in Europe remains to be seen.

What can be patented

Existing principles

As will be mentioned in Chapter 5.1, the general requirements for patentability, those of novelty, inventive step and industrial applicability, apply to biotechnological inventions as to any other areas of technology. The requirements for novelty and industrial applicability are of particular interest for biotechnological inventions:

- *Invention or mere discovery?* Biotechnological inventions often involve the characterization and isolation of elements existing in nature, such as biological material. It has long been accepted, however, that discoveries are not patentable. Opponents to patents for, for example, genes encoding human proteins have argued that such things are mere discoveries and therefore unpatentable. The law does not agree. According to the EU Directive, as long as the material is isolated from its natural environment, or is produced by means of a technical process, it may be patented, even if it previously occurred in nature.
- *New use for a known substance?* This is a 'wrinkle' in the law of patents that is of particular interest and relevance to those concerned with pharmaceuticals. It is possible to obtain patent protection for the use as a medicament of a known substance. Thus, for example, if it is found that a substance known previously only as a food colour has activity in the treatment of a disease condition, that 'first medical use' is regarded as new and can be patented, even though the substance *per se* was previously known. Furthermore, if it is then found that that same substance has a second medical use, that too can be protected, as long as the claim to the substance is limited by a statement to the new use. In the pharmaceutical industry, screening known, off-patent medicaments for new medicinal uses is a strategy used by companies to get products to market quickly, short circuiting the usual process of obtaining regulatory approval.
- *Industrially applicable?* The requirement for industrial applicability has been used to disqualify from patentability methods for treatment of the human or animal body by surgery or therapy, and diagnostic methods practised on the human or animal body. Public policy considerations

clearly drove the introduction of this exception, which interestingly is not present in US law, although in that jurisdiction a recent amendment to US law exempts medical practitioners and health care entities from infringement liability for the performance of patented medical procedures that do not involve drugs or devices.

Specific provisions

In addition to the existing requirements mentioned above, patent laws contain specific provisions that affirm or restrict the patentability of certain types of biotechnological invention. The main restrictions are:

■ *Patents for animals and plants?* European patent law states explicitly that plant and animal varieties cannot be patented. This is somewhat misleading. It does not mean that patents cannot be obtained for plants and animals, but in the case of plants at least, this provision exists in the law simply to prevent a conflict arising between European patent law and national laws for the protection of plant varieties (see above). The European Patent Office has approved the grant of a patent for the Harvard onco-mouse, with a claim that it is a transgenic, thus, the principle has been established that transgenic animals are patentable in Europe. The EPO's position on plants, is that it is possible to obtain broad patent claims to transgenic plants, as long as the claims are not directed to specific plant varieties. It is worth noting that patents with claims to transgenic non-human mammals have been being granted in both the United States and Japan for a number of years.

■ *Is it an 'essentially biological' process?* An 'essentially biological' process has been defined as one that consists entirely of natural phenomena such as crossing or selection. Such processes cannot be patented in Europe.

■ *Can human beings be patented?* The EU Directive says that the following are not patentable:
  - processes for cloning human beings;
  - processes for modifying the germ line genetic identity of human beings;
  - uses of human embryos for industrial or commercial purposes;
  - the human body, at the various stages of its formation and development, and the simple discovery of one of its elements, including the sequence or partial sequence of a gene.

Here again it can be seen that considerations of public policy and morality have been at work. These provisions are relatively new and little in the way of guidance as to their meaning is available.

■ *Is it moral?* There is a great deal of debate in the IP world over whether or not patent laws should contain provisions restricting the patenting of inventions that society regards as immoral. In practice it is patent office examiners, not politicians, who are faced with the prospect of applying these provisions. Should they have to carry the burden of making decisions about what is or is not moral, and are they in fact qualified to do so? The situation at present is that the EU Directive prohibits the patenting of 'processes for modifying the genetic identity of animals which are likely to cause them suffering without any substantial medical benefit to man or animal, and also animals resulting from such processes'. For example, it is possible to genetically modify a rat to carry a human cancer gene, in order to better facilitate the study of that cancer *in vivo*. If the rat suffers as a result, one has to balance its suffering with the potential benefits to human anti-cancer medicine in deciding if the rat is patentable, and this issue was debated extensively in the Harvard onco-mouse case at the EPO (referred to above).

Affirmations

■ *Biological material.* The EU Directive defines biological material as 'any material containing genetic information and capable of reproducing itself or being reproduced in a biological system', and goes on to affirm explicitly that the following are patentable:
  – biological material that is isolated from its natural environment or produced by means of a technical process even if it previously occurred in nature;
  – plants or animals if the technical feasibility of the invention is not confined to a particular plant or animal variety;
  – a microbiological or other technical process, or a product obtained by means of such a process other than a plant or animal variety.
■ *Human beings again.* Although the majority of the new provisions that relate to patents and human beings are proscriptive, it is explicitly affirmed that an element isolated from the human body or otherwise produced by means of a technical process, including the sequence or partial sequence of a gene, may constitute a patentable invention, even if the structure of that element is identical to that of a natural element.

A complex and rapidly changing area

The process of applying for, and obtaining grant of, valid and commercially useful patents for biotechnological inventions is a complicated one, made more so by the number of additional rules and regulations and the changing practices of patent offices that apply to this technical area. As such, professional assistance is crucial if costly mistakes are to be avoided.

As an illustration of this general proposition, it appears that for biotechnology inventions, in recent years patent offices have become increasingly strict in applying the rules that require that the monopoly that is claimed is actually merited by the technical disclosure in the patent application. In practice what this means is that more technical data must be produced at an early stage to show that the invention works over the claimed scope than was previously required, or than may be required to get broad patent protection in other technical areas. A failure to provide the necessary data can result in the grant of claims of only limited scope, and only limited commercial value.

Reuben Jacob is a Chartered Patent Agent and European Patent Attorney and heads up the life sciences department of R G C Jenkins & Co in London. His background is in microbiology and genetics, and his particular interest and expertise lies in helping UK biotech clients with the acquisition of intellectual property rights. His contact details are: Reuben E. Jacob, R G C Jenkins & Co, 26 Caxton Street, London SW1H 0RJ; tel: +44 (0) 20 7931 7141; fax: +44 (0) 20 7222 4660; e-mail: rjacob@jenkins-ip.com; Web site: www.jenkins-ip.com

Universities

Good IP management is not just financially important to universities. It also contributes to other key university aims and objectives, such as the generation, application and transfer of knowledge.

The public profile of UK higher education is arguably higher than at any time in its history, and while there is intense debate about how the sector should be funded, there is also unprecedented consensus about the vital contribution universities make to the economy and society. Our higher education institutions equip people with high-level skills, and through their research and knowledge transfer activities generate and apply new knowledge to enhance economic prosperity and quality of life. Their success in this regard depends increasingly on the effective management of intellectual property (IP) generated through their various activities, for which they need to have appropriate strategies and policies in place.

Why IP is management important to universities

Virtually all university teaching and research activities give rise to IP which is, in principle, exploitable for example through its sale and licensing, including the establishment of spin-out companies. Good IP management is important, not only because of the financial returns that it can help to generate, but because it also contributes to other key university aims and objectives, such as the generation, application and transfer of knowledge.

Shared investment, shared benefits

The commercialization of IP can generate income, although all involved need to be realistic over the scale of returns. These are uncertain and typically realized over the medium to long term, with significant up-front investment and acceptance of a lengthy pay-back period usually required.

A large proportion of university research is carried out in collaboration with sponsors, frequently leading to complex issues in managing IP. Many universities prefer to own the IP arising from the sponsored research, but ultimately ownership is decided by negotiation between the parties. Agreements between the different parties seek to ensure that:

■ potential conflicts of interest are recognized and accommodated;
■ returns to each party reflect their inputs to the project;
■ university staff are able to use the results in future research.

Universities are also concerned to ensure that agreements are framed so that the financial interests of universities, and individual researchers, do not compromise either academic freedom or their institutional independence.

Knowledge transfer

A central part of universities' work is the generation and application of knowledge and its transfer to users in the public and private sectors. Disseminating openly, and making results freely available, through publication in academic journals, will often be the most effective way of achieving this. However, most research outputs require significant additional investment before they can be brought to market. Such investments may only be commercially attractive if the underpinning research results are protected, thereby restricting competition. This protection need not prevent publication, although it might cause short delays in publication as patents are filed.

Other collaboration opportunities

As well as collaboration between universities and sponsors, there are also benefits in collaboration between universities, or between research teams spread across different universities, that businesses may wish to consider. For example:

■ Joint marketing of IP portfolios might be cost-effective.
■ A single university can bring together IP from different departments, but the potential to create high-value packages is greater if the scope of the research is wider.

■ Collaboration might enable a group of universities to employ sector or technology specialists dedicated to enhancing the effectiveness of IP management.

Even universities with large IP portfolios and well-staffed IP management offices do not always expect to have all the required expertise in-house. They may use external legal specialists and patent attorneys as required, and may also seek advice and/or services from IP management providers.

Students and staff

Incentives can be an important part in encouraging staff and students to play a part in exploiting IP. Formula-based schemes for sharing revenue between the university and inventors are well established. Opportunities to supplement university salaries through commercialization, are an increasingly important consideration for many academics. Incentives may also extend beyond financial benefits: for example, consideration of IP-related activities as a criterion for promotion can also be important.

Although they have a role in its exploitation, universities do not legally have an automatic claim to IP generated by their students. In some instances therefore, students may be treated at least on the same basis as staff, in order to encourage them to use university IP management resources.

Monitoring IP management

There is a need to monitor performance in IP management, as this can help to identify problems and opportunities, and allow university managers to modify budgets and strategies accordingly. The long time lags between costs incurred and revenues received mean that those evaluating financial performance should be patient.

Universities often seek to ensure that IP management is integrated with other management activities in order to create an environment in which researchers can come forward with ideas. This also helps to ensure that university staff are aware of IP issues.

Universities' commitment to IP management

Universities are committed to ensuring that researchers within institutions can access expert advice, and that those same experts encourage researchers to explore the potential for exploitation of research outcomes. All UK universities provide such advice through specialist liaison officers and enterprise units. The UK government has recognized the value of their work in this area, and provides support towards provision of these facilities alongside other so-called 'third stream' activities.

As well as on-site facilities, the UK community also has a good base of written information. In 2002, Universities UK – with the UK Patent Office and the Association for University Research and Industry Links (AURIL) – published *Managing Intellectual Property: A guide to strategic decision-making*. Much of the advice in this chapter is based upon the information contained within this guide. Copies are available from Universities UK.

Universities UK is the representative body for the executive heads of all UK universities. It works to advance the interests of universities and to spread good practice throughout the higher education sector. Its mission is to be the essential voice of UK universities by promoting and supporting their work.

Universities UK works to achieve a vision of UK universities that are autonomous, properly funded from a diversity of sources, accessible to all, delivering high-quality teaching and learning, and at the leading edge of research of regional, national and international significance. It provides information and advice to its 122 members on all issues affecting them, including the management of intellectual property. For further information on Universities UK please visit www.universitiesuk.ac.uk or if you have any queries or questions, e-mail: info@universitiesuk.ac.uk

5
Defining rights

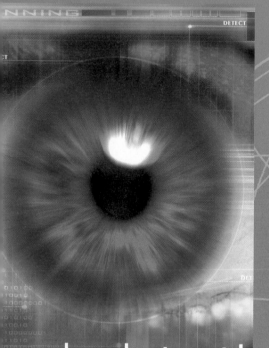

Patents

Dr Jeremy Philpott of the Patent Office discusses the process of securing exclusive rights to an invention.

Among the earliest patents were those granted to glass makers in the 1420s by the State of Venice, and the first known English patent was granted in 1449 to a Flemish glass maker attracted to England to make the stained glass windows for the chapel at Eton College. The term of the patent was long enough for John of Utynam to train two generations of apprentices but not have them compete against him (by virtue of his patent), so as to encourage him to pass on his secrets rather than take them to his grave. Down the ages patent terms have varied between 14 and 20 years, reflecting this basic principle.

Patents are often regarded as the 'crown jewels' of the intellectual property system, and they can certainly cost more than jewels do! Innovation is seen to be driven forward by the patent system in three important ways:

- the provision by the state of exclusive rights to inventors encourages them to invest in research and development (R&D), confident that they can enjoy revenue from their new invention;
- the publication of the invention's details in a patent enables other researchers to focus their efforts on new improvements rather than tackling problems that have already been solved by others;
- limiting the lifetime of a patent (to a maximum of 20 years) means no inventor is able to rest on his or her laurels – knowing that competitors will

be able to use the information in a patent once it expires motivates patentees to come up with further inventions to maintain their market lead.

For an invention to be worthy of patent protection it must be new, non-obvious and useful. These three features are known in the legislation as:

■ *Novelty.* The invention must not previously be known in the public domain anywhere in the world prior to the filing date of the patent application. If someone else has previously invented the same or similar technology, and disclosed it, the patent application will fail. If the inventor has disclosed how the invention works to others without an obligation of confidence (see Chapter 5.5), the patent application will be invalid. Note that it might be safe to disclose what an invention does (for example, 'My invention halves production times for product X – would you like to buy a licence?') provided it is not implicit as to how it is achieved. (Beware of differences in the US system on this point, both in terms of a 'grace period', which permits disclosure prior to patent filing, and the notion that the rightful owner of the patent to an invention is the first to invent, not the first to file. See Chapter 1.4.)

■ *Inventive step.* The invention must not be a mere combination of known features amounting to an entirely expected result. If an inventor combines a dog-lead with a torch the result is a device useful for walking a dog at night. If no technological barrier had to be overcome in combining those features, and the end product is no more than the sum of its parts, there is no invention. The term 'obvious' comes from the Latin *ob via* – 'lying in the road', and refers to those solutions that are just waiting to be stumbled across while following a straight line from the problem to the solution. Conversely, selecting the ideal solution from a large numbers of options can be inventive. Similarly an invention can be the discovery of an advantage from a combination of known features which gives greater than expected benefits: the invention is greater than the sum of its parts. Furthermore, going against a technical prejudice can also be inventive. For example, if all the textbooks say that a chemical process is best performed below 500 °C, and indeed that above this temperature the process will not work, it would be inventive to discover that at above 800 °C the process can usefully be performed for an even better yield. (In this last example the discovery is that contaminating by-products are prevalent between 500 and 800 °C, but no one had previously thought to explore a yet higher temperature regime.) It is not advisable to let the geniuses in an R&D team judge what is 'inventive' and what is not – to them everything seems obvious because they are so immersed in the technological chase that they often cannot appreciate a breakthrough for what it is.

■ *Industrial application.* The invention must have a use, even if it is only a toy or game. No patent office requires working models, nor does any have laboratories where they verify the claims of patent applicants about the efficacy of their inventions. The patent examiners have to take the applicant's experimental data at face value. However, those inventions that manifestly do not work (such as perpetual motion machines) are refused patent protection. The requirement that an invention has a use excludes pure discoveries from patent protection. This means that the discovery of penicillin (a naturally occurring substance) was not itself patentable, although patents were granted when it was worked up into a shelf-stable form for use as an antibiotic (namely a useful application for the discovery, rather than for the discovery itself).

A further criterion applied to the patent application (as opposed to the invention itself) is that the disclosure must be 'sufficient'. The patent system exists, among other reasons, to disseminate information, so all patents must contain enough information to allow others to repeat the invention. It is assumed that the patent is addressed to other skilled readers: a background of relevant knowledge is taken for granted. But the specifics of the invention must be explained, so that others working in the same field understand how to repeat the invention either under licence or after the patent expires, and know the extent of the rights covered by the patent. (Chapter 5.5 discusses the boundaries of sufficiency with technological know-how.)

The exceptions

It is important to note that certain 'inventions' (in the loosest sense of the word) are not protected by patents. The exclusions from patent protection include:

■ Mere mental acts like arithmetic or book-keeping, whether they are done in a human brain or in a computer.
■ The presentation of information – road signs, marker buoys, odometers which flash when a vehicle is due for a service, a gambling machine with a variety of logos instead of fruit symbols on the three barrels – all of these are not true inventions. Patents in this area must relate to technical features independent of the information being conveyed.
■ Artistic creations, along with literary, musical and dramatic works are protected by copyright (see Chapter 5.3) and are thereby excluded from patent protection. However, do not let this blind you to the technical merits of seemingly aesthetic matters of colour or shape which might confer patentability on a product. The shape of a gear tooth might make it more hard-wearing (a technical benefit, and hence patentable if it is novel). A squash ball was once patented simply because it was blue: aside

from its aesthetics, the applicants brought evidence that the human eye is better able to track a fast-moving blue ball than a fast-moving black ball, hence their product had a technical advantage.

■ Methods of playing a game – you should win a game of tennis because you are better player, not because your opponent may not use the 'drop volley' due to your patent.

■ Methods of doing business – for the same reason as the exclusion above against methods of playing a game, it is felt that innovative business methods like discount schemes for loyal customers, financial transactions, or online retail, should succeed in the market place on their own merits, not because competitors are forbidden from trading in the same way. Note the divergence of practice on this point between Europe and the United States (see Chapter 1.4).

■ Computer programs – in isolation 10,000 lines of code have no use whatsoever (that is, they lack industrial application). However, an estimated 15 per cent of patent applications relate to computer-implemented inventions, many of which are granted, because they disclose not just the software, but the context in which it is used. So while a program listing is not patentable, a device that uses that program to achieve an effect (such as guide a missile to its target, route callers through a telephone exchange, or improve the operational speed of a computer) is eminently patentable. Such patents therefore embrace the objectives of the software (for example, as an eight-step flow diagram) and afford exclusivity to the patentee irrespective of the details of the underlying code, or even what language it was written in. (For more detail on these issues see Chapter 4.5.)

■ Methods of treatment, surgery or diagnosis for humans or animals – there is an overriding public policy concern that no patient requiring treatment should be denied it because a physician cannot obtain permission from a patentee to use, for example, a new surgical technique. Nevertheless medical implements (such as heart pacemakers, prosthetic limbs and ultrasound scanners) and new medications may be patented, just not the methods by which they are used.

■ As noted above with reference to penicillin, mere discoveries lacking an industrial application are not patentable. Likewise mathematical equations and scientific theories (such as Darwin's theory of evolution) are unpatentable. However, discoveries become patentable when a use can be identified. Most recently this has been seen with biotechnology, where genes have been isolated and used in a host of applications. Although the genes themselves are not novel (they have existed in nature for millennia) there has often been inventive merit in isolating the genes (they do not exist in nature in isolation, but as part of the DNA strand), and then making use of them in diagnosis or therapy. In this sense genes are patentable because once isolated they are novel and have a use.

■ Offensive or immoral inventions – more specifically this relates to inventions that, if commercially exploited, would cause an outcry. Human cloning is excluded under this term, as would devices that facilitate torture. The Ottawa Convention 1998 outlawed anti-personnel landmines, and hence these too fall into this exclusion. It is important to note, however, that just because something is illegal, it does not necessarily follow that it is immoral. Police chiefs have, in the past, decried the use of radar jamming devices used by persistent speeding motorists seeking to defy speed cameras, but their complaints that patents should not have been granted for such devices were in vain. Just because it might be illegal to use a device in one country, it does not mean that its manufacture should not be patented, especially if the device is then to be exported to a country where its use is permitted.

Professional help

No one would dream of acquiring something as expensive as a house without the advice of a solicitor. So it is with patents. The law allows inventors to file applications on their own, and so-called 'private applicants' make up almost a quarter of all patent applicants in the UK. However, their applications have a higher than average attrition rate, and the few patents that get granted (just 8 per cent or less) are often not renewed, or are not commercially viable. Anyone who is serious about securing the best possible protection for an invention is likely to use a patent attorney. Their fees range from a few hundred to several thousand pounds, depending on the complexity of the technology and the amount of help that is needed. In the UK it is possible to find one of these experts through their professional body, the Chartered Institute of Patent Agents.

The patenting process

When first filed a patent application must contain a description and all the relevant diagrams required to understand and replicate the invention, and to distinguish it from earlier inventions. If the invention is reliant on a special technical detail to distinguish it from similar ones found in the subsequent search, and that essential detail is absent from the description, it may not be added at a later stage.

By the end of the first year it is necessary need to file an abstract (short summary), claims, and pay for a search, but these can be filed earlier with the description and diagrams. The claims are the legally enforced part of a patent, defining precisely what others are excluded from doing. They must be 'supported' by the description – this means that claims to a novel compound used in brake linings will not be allowed in a patent whose description only discloses the construction of the brake callipers.

The search report will list any citations (patents or technical papers) that show that the invention as claimed was previously known – these are 'prior art'. Some documents will stand alone to injure the alleged novelty of the application; other related documents will be read together to show that the invention is obvious or lacks 'inventive step' – that it is merely a combination of known features.

The patent application and the search report will be published if the applicant wishes to proceed to examination. Publication of the 'A' specification (so called because the serial number ends in the letter 'A' – this convention is used in many countries) gives the public a chance to see what the technology is all about. The published application can now be used as a citation against subsequent patents filed by others to disprove their novelty. Competitors will know what the applicant is doing, but they will also be put on notice that he, she or it is hoping to acquire exclusive rights on a new technology. If a patent is later granted it is possible to sue infringers for actions begun after the 'A' publication date, even if done before grant, because publication told them 'keep out – patent pending'. This publication also gives the public, particularly competitors, a chance to make observations on the validity of the application. Although third parties may not become involved in the patent examination process, they may file evidence (for example, more prior art) to be used by the examiner in his or her considerations.

The examination process can involve several exchanges of correspondence between the examiner and the applicant (or his or her patent attorney). Using the prior art the examiner will seek to restrict the scope of the claims to only cover those aspects of the invention that are novel and inventive. So a patent application that once claimed rights in 'an electric kettle' might be reduced to claiming only 'an electric kettle characterized by a ceramic heating element that is integral to the base plate' (assuming that, first, even this feature is novel and inventive, and second, the description had this detail in the first place!). Other legal proofreading is done, and the applicant or his/her attorney has the right to argue against the examiner's views until the patent is in a final form agreeable to both sides. At this point the patent is granted and republished (so-called 'B' publication). It may now be used in court in the event of an infringement.

Foreign filings

A UK patent provides exclusive rights only in the UK. Given that patent applications are published to be seen around the world, there is nothing to stop a foreign company reading a UK patent application and copying the invention abroad – unless the patentee also has patents in other countries. One-third of UK patent applications come from foreign firms wishing to protect their UK market.

Over 100 countries are party to an agreement that allows 'equivalent' patent applications to be filed abroad up to one year after the domestic patent filing date. This protocol, known as the 'priority period', ensures that foreign applications are treated as if they had been filed in the other countries on the same filing date as the first domestic filing date (the so-called 'priority date'). This is important because any disclosure of the invention before a patent's filing date will invalidate a subsequent application. So if an applicant was to file a patent application in the UK, and then start to openly discuss or sell the invention, subsequent patent applications filed abroad would have filing dates after the disclosures, and hence be invalid. Thankfully, the 'priority year' protocol means that provided those foreign filings are made within a year of the first patent filing they will be afforded the same effective 'priority date' which, crucially, predates any disclosures made after the first filing. This enables individuals and organizations to test foreign markets or seek foreign licensing deals before committing resources to foreign patent applications.

There is an international patent application system (the Patent Co-operation Treaty (PCT)) to which almost every country is a signatory. This provides an applicant with up to 30 months in which to decide in which markets it wishes to pursue protection. This gives time to test foreign markets, and find the money for subsequent translations. Initially the application is handled in a single language by a central authority (the World Intellectual Property Organization (WIPO) in Geneva), and a single search report is issued with regard to relevant citations ('prior art'). If the applicant decides to proceed with the application, it needs to file translations into the languages of every country in which it wishes to acquire protection, then its applications are examined under the national patent laws of each country. If granted, the rights are national, and a challenge to the patent in one state has no bearing on its validity in another.

Similarly, over 30 European States are contracting States to the European Patent Organization, whose head office, the European Patent Office (EPO) is based in Munich. At the EPO a single application in English, French or German is searched, published, examined and granted. Anyone (typically a competitor) can bring evidence, eg to support an 'opposition' in the first nine months following grant. That is, it can claim that the applicant cannot have rights over the invention because it has evidence, eg the invention was not novel prior to its filing date. If the patent survives opposition, it then proliferates into a bundle of discrete national rights, taking effect when translations are lodged at the patent offices of the relevant States. As with PCT patents (above), the final granted patents are separate, and any litigation takes places in national courts with no bearing on related rights in other countries.

The European Community Patent has been discussed at great length, but negotiations are far from complete. The intention is to create a patent covering the whole of the European Union, to be granted and litigated as a single entity. In comparison with the EPO route, where the loss of one patent in a court action means that over a dozen equivalent patents remain in other countries, the Community Patent would produce an 'all or nothing' result in the event of litigation. For the Community Patent to become a reality there needs to be agreement between the member states on who will process the applications, which court should hear any disputes, and what language regime should prevail. On this last point it is worth noting that minimizing any requirement for translations is vital in reducing costs to patentees.

Costs

The UK Patent Office is unusual in that it does not charge an initial filing fee. The total fees covering things like search, publication, examination and grant amount to only £200. These fees are kept low so as to minimize costs to inventors at the early stages of developing their products or processes. However, this does not mean that acquiring a patent is cheap. As noted above, using a patent attorney could cost several thousand pounds, and organizations might need attorneys in other countries to prosecute their foreign filings, which have their own attendant filing fees and translation costs. It has recently been estimated that for an 'average' invention (as opposed to a deeply complex biotechnology or telecommunications invention), acquiring patent rights in the United States would cost £6,500. When translation costs are added on this rises to £10,400 for Japan and £31,700 for eight European countries via the EPO. Thankfully these costs are spread over the two to six years (or longer) it takes to get a patent granted in multiple countries, but if the applicant is not making substantial income from the invention by the time these bills roll in, he, she or it might be better off abandoning the patent before it consumes any more cash.

Once granted, patents are kept in force by the payment of annual renewal fees. In the UK these fees cover the loss the Patent Office makes in handling applications that are unsuccessful. Patents may be renewed up to the maximum patent lifetime of 20 years, calculated from the filing date, not the grant date. Only about 5 per cent of patents are renewed right up to their 20th year. For example, in automotive engineering some technologies are obsolete after 10 years, so patentees no longer need to pay to protect the exclusivity in technologies that have been superseded. If the patentee chooses to stop paying renewal fees, the patent becomes free for anyone to use and the patentee may not restore the patent by resuming payments.

Co-inventors

It should already be clear that in collaborating with others prior to patent filing it is essential to have a confidentiality agreement. Equally vital, however, but too easy to overlook, is an agreement to cover ownership of any intellectual property (especially a patent) arising from the collaboration. An inventor might confidentially approach an engineering firm to develop prototypes of a device, and then lawfully apply for a patent. But he or she could be stuck when he/she discovers that the firm has filed a patent application for the device that makes the product!

What happens if that firm not only makes that prototype to the original specification but also develops an improved version? The originator will now want the better version, but the firm will also have patent rights as co-inventors. The invention process can take participants in many different directions, and can lead to input from unexpected sources, so it is important to plan accordingly. Contracts that deal with ownership of the evolving invention should be drafted before commercialization begins to avoid unwanted claims for rights in the invention.

Using a patent

Too many inventors think that a patent is an end in itself, rather than realize that it is a means to an end. Having a patent will not, of itself, make any money. This property right needs to be worked, just like a house that only makes money if it has tenants in it. Other chapters of this book explain in more detail such subjects as licensing (Chapters 2.5 and 2.6) and raising venture capital (Chapter 3.5). Indeed, patent applications can be great tools to attract investors; it is vital to be sure that getting the patents granted does not consume all those funds!

Even for those who do not own a patent, the information contained in patents makes for a goldmine of technical and commercial intelligence (see Chapter 2.3). Just having a patent published helps to put a company on the map, and might attract potential business allies who discover the patent in a database and want to work with its creator. Another benefit is that having a patent application published will prevent any future patent application for the same invention being granted – this will deny rivals any exclusive rights in that area even if the original patent is not granted. For many small firms it is more important that they deny anyone else exclusivity than it is for them to control exclusivity themselves. Wilfully disclosing a technology (ideally through patents, but otherwise through technical journals and the like) so as to 'spoil' the later patenting ambitions of others is a perfectly viable business strategy – and very inexpensive!

As can be seen, patents have more uses than simply to litigate against trespassers (see Part 6). Given that patents have so many different uses, it helps to keep a cool head when faced with an infringement. Before serving writs consider this – could the market share lost to the infringers be recovered by investing in more aggressive marketing, and would this cost less than it would cost to take them to court? Could the organization buy the infringing company for less than it would cost to sue them? All civil litigation is expensive, so it should be used as a last resort and with extreme care.

For more information about any aspect of IP, visit www.patent.gov.uk or call 08459 500 505.

Trade marks

Dr Jeremy Philpott of the Patent Office discusses legal protection for reputations and brands.

Reputations take years to build, and the strength of a brand is often a business's most valuable asset. Once its customers trust its products and services, they will be more willing to try other goods it offers them in the future. How they come to recognize an organization in the market, and distinguish it from competitors, is crucial. Seemingly everyone knows what a trade mark is, but surprisingly few small or new businesses understand how to lever them for best effect.

Unregistered trade marks

Any trader who finds that a competitor is using the same or a similar name in trade, so as to confuse or divert customers, can bring a so-called 'passing off' action under common law. Where a name has acquired a reputation in a locality or market sector it can be regarded as an 'unregistered' trade mark – a right arises automatically as a result of its use in trade. To be successful in an action it is necessary to prove to the court that the organization has acquired goodwill in the mark, that the other party is acting so as to confuse its customers, and that harm has been, or is likely to be, done to its trade. Examples of futile passing-off actions include:

- suing a company with the same name in another distant town if the plaintiff's services are local to its own town (that is, there is no commonality between its customer base and that of the alleged infringer);
- suing a company trading under a person's name (such as Mary's Florists) if that is the trader's own name, and it is the same as the plaintiff's by coincidence;
- suing a company whose name is directly descriptive of what it does (such as Kwik Cabs), and it started trading before the plaintiff established a reputation.

In short, unregistered marks, as a 'soft' right, are effortless to create but difficult and onerous to enforce. They may optionally be denoted by the symbol 'TM', although some IP lawyers snigger that this stands for 'totally meaningless', and that the only protection worth having comes through registration. If someone else gets a registration before the organization does, it might find itself geographically 'fenced in'. For example, imagine if a bookshop in Derby had been calling itself 'Amazon' since the 1970s, without ever seeking a registration. During the 1990s the successful Amazon® online book retailer has acquired trade mark registrations for the UK. That shop in Derby would be allowed to continue trading on the basis of established 'prior use', but given that its reputation only extends to a customer base in Derby, that is where it would now be trapped. It would not be allowed to open a second branch in another town under the same name without the permission of the owner of the registered trade mark – the better-known online retailer.

Registered trade marks

A registered trade mark is a 'badge of origin' telling consumers where goods or services have come from. Once it is registered, the owner can prevent anyone else from using the same or similar word, logo or sign in relation to trade in the same or similar goods and services as its own registration. The owner is also allowed to use the ® symbol. (To do so without a registration is an offence.)

Registration provides greater legal certainty, but not everything is registrable. Traditionally, ordinary words or logos have made the best registered trade marks, but it is vital to avoid the common trap of naming a business after either the proprietor, the type of trade, or the location. 'Fred Jones Second Hand Cars, Leicester' is a disaster in trade mark terms. The law allows anyone to trade under his or her own name, irrespective of trade mark rights owned by another, so such a mark would not be enforceable against anyone else called 'Fred Jones'. Indeed people's surnames are often difficult to register, especially if they are very common (one test is to see if the name occurs frequently in the London phone book).

Trade marks are not allowed by law to be directly descriptive of the goods – this means that a grocer may not have the exclusive right to the words 'apple' or 'orange', although they have been registered as trade marks for unrelated goods and services such as music, computers and telecommunications. Geographical terms struggle to become trade marks – no single trader should have exclusivity over the use of, for instance, a town's or a shire's name. However PGIs, as mentioned in Chapter 1.3, may be suitable in such instances, for example Parma ham, or champagne.

While some catchy slogans become more memorable than the brand itself, it must be remembered that laudatory terms (like 'superior', 'best', 'premier', 'excellent') may not be registered because all traders seek to use such terms in their marketing hype. So the organization should take care in choosing a slogan that it might wish to register at a later date – if it can be distinctive without being descriptive or laudatory it has the best chance of being registered. 'The best sportswear in the world' will stumble where 'Just do it ®' prevails.

The best marks are those that are distinctive yet meaningless, either because they are invented words, or because they bear no relation to the goods or services to which they are applied. Dulux® products are evoked just by seeing a shaggy Old English sheepdog, yet the dog itself is not a paint. Consider Richard Branson's far-reaching brand 'Virgin®'. By picking a distinctive term which was not descriptive of the record industry, he created a brand capable of diversifying into holidays, finance and travel. Would you really want to board a transatlantic jet emblazoned with the words 'Richard's Records'? No, I thought not.

If the organization is lucky its branding will extend beyond just names and logos into colours, shapes, sounds or even gestures. The colour purple is synonymous with Cadburys® in relation to chocolate, but with Silk Cut® in relation to cigarettes. This does not mean that no one may use that tone of purple to paint a house or dye clothes – it just means that those colours may only be used by the brand owners in relation to trade in chocolate or cigarettes respectively. Music of all sorts is used in advertising, and once it becomes distinctive of a trader it is registrable in relation to its goods or services – but the music itself may still be played by others provided they do not do so in a related trade context. (Note that the music is likely to be protected by copyright, and so the trade mark owner will need to acquire the rights in the rendition used.) Anyone can use a triangular prism to sell a product – unless it is chocolate, in which case the seller will have to answer to Toblerone®. Likewise, we are all capable of patting our back pocket (such that loose change rattles), but only Asda® may do so in promoting its retail services. When seeking to register such unconventional marks, the organization might be asked to prove that the public sees such signs as being its distinctive 'badge of origin'. Getting such proof (for instance, through customer surveys) can be difficult and expensive.

Even if a mark is initially refused a registration because it lacks distinctiveness, through tireless exploitation in the market place it can 'acquire distinctiveness through use' and become registrable at a later date. The sooner the mark becomes distinctive the sooner it can be registered, so it is important to choose wisely. Conversely, if an organization does not use its trade mark in the market in connection with any of the goods or services for which it was registered for more than five years, then the mark risks becoming unenforceable (despite the registration) in relation to those goods or services.

It is crucial to check, before the organization starts trading, that the name or other sign for the business or product has not already been registered by another organization. The Trade Marks Register can be searched for free from the Patent Office Web site (see Chapter 2.3). Once the organization is sure that its trading name does not infringe an earlier registered trade mark, it should consider registering it as a trade mark before anyone else does. Advice on registration issues for a specific mark can be obtained from the Patent Office's Trade Mark Search and Advisory Service (a commercial service), and employing a trade mark attorney could be invaluable.

Foreign filings

As with patents, registered trade marks are distinct territorial rights, and so registrations must be sought in every country that forms part of the organization's market. In the UK, a registration will cost £200 in a single class of trade, plus £50 for each additional class (for example, £300 to protect a logo in three classes, if it is displayed on clothing, mugs and magazines as part of the merchandising of a pop music band). A registration lasts for 10 years, whereupon it is renewable at 10-yearly intervals.

The European Union has a central trade marks registry based in Alicante in Spain. The Office for Harmonization in the Internal Market (OHIM) provides a single trade mark registration enforceable across every EU Member State. The OHIM and the UK Patent Office apply exactly the same criteria when considering trade mark applications. Of course, if during the registration process it emerges that a mark is (for example) descriptive of a well-known place name in any one of the member states, the application will be refused, leaving the applicant to fall back on applying to individual national registries in the other States.

The World Intellectual Property Organization (WIPO) based in Geneva operates the so-called 'Madrid System' for international trade mark applications. Like the PCT for patents (see Chapter 5.1), this scheme allows a single application to be handled initially, before proliferating into a bundle of national applications to be registered under the laws of the various nations. Over 60 countries are party to the Madrid Protocol, including the United States, Japan, the UK and most European states. By the end of 2004 the EU itself (in the sense of a Community trade mark from OHIM) will be an entity that applicants can designate on their Madrid applications.

A professional trade mark attorney will be able to advise applicants on all their options with regard to trade mark applications, both at home and abroad.

Domain names

Registering a company name at Companies House is not the same as registering a trade mark. Likewise, domain name registration is an entirely separate matter. However, it is worth noting that incorporating another person's trade marks into a domain name or into the metatags of a Web site can land the organization in very hot water. If its own domain name is not the same as it trade mark, it might well be advisable to register the URL as a trade mark itself. Given that squabbles over domain names when resolved by Nominet or the ICANN can only result in cancellation, transfer or freezing of the offending Web site, it can be preferable to sue under trade mark law to recover damages if the organization has lost business to a cyber-squatter.

For more information about any aspect of IP visit www.patent.gov.uk or call 08459 500 505.

Copyright

Although the principle of copyright law has stood up to 300 years of techno-logical change, says Dr Jeremy Philpott at the Patent Office, disputes over how rights apply will continue to arise.

Prior to the Renaissance the written word was exclusively controlled by the Church, the State and the wealthy educated classes. The advent of the printing press changed all that, and the distribution of written ideas to the masses that might be seditious worried the establishment so much that it passed the first copyright law 300 years ago. In truth it was really a mech-anism for State control over which (approved) books could be published, but it established the notion of property in ideas. Over time this principle of copyright has been extended to music, artwork and dramatic perform-ances, and has proven remarkably flexible. Once music was only protected by the copyright in sheet music, and when the gramophone recording was invented people said that copyright law was dead. Then came radio, which played such recordings, and again they said copyright law was dead. Then came the twin-cassette deck which facilitated home taping of music, and again they said copyright law was dead. In truth, the law has proven to be flexible and adaptable, matching or even anticipating changes in tech-nology. Now that music can be digitized and files transferred over the Internet it has again been said that copyright law is dead, but the track record of such prophets is poor!

It is important to remember that copyright relates to the expression of an idea, not the idea itself. Conceiving a new tune in your mind does not give rise to any copyright, nor does humming it, singing it or playing it on an

WILSON GUNN

PATENT & TRADE MARK ATTORNEYS

Serving clients in Intellectual Property
matters for over 100 years

Visit our website
www.wilsongunn.com

E-mail
enquiries@wilsongunn.com

Charles House,	Chancery House,	5th Floor, Blackfriars House,
148/9 Great Charles Street,	Chancery Lane,	The Parsonage,
Birmingham,	London,	Manchester,
B3 3HT	WC2A 1QU	M3 2JA
Tel: 0121 236 1038	Tel: 0207 242 2631	Tel: 0161 827 9400
Fax: 0121 233 2875	Fax: 0207 242 0075	Fax: 0161 832 4905

BIRMINGHAM - LONDON - MANCHESTER

instrument. However, when the expressed idea becomes 'fixed', either by ink on a page (for example, a score), or recorded onto magnetic or digital media, then copyright is enjoyed in that recording. The clearest example of this is a cake recipe in a book. Copyright protects the words on the page: no one else may write them out or photocopy that page without permission. However, to bake the cake as instructed by the recipe is not an infringement of the copyright of the written words. There is a common fallacy among some business people that copyright will protect something as vague as a business plan (perhaps for a new sales promotion campaign) if it is simply written down. In truth only the words on the page are protected by copyright, not the business plan itself. Such business plans are protected (if at all) by the laws on trade secrecy and confidentiality – see Chapter 5.5.

A 'literary work' might be a novel, or something as short as a poem, a verse or even a sentence. However, an isolated word, name or title is not a 'literary work' *per se*, and hence not protected by copyright. This is why the author J K Rowling, despite having copyright in her *Harry Potter* children's novels, has sought trade mark registration for the titles of the novels and for the names of key characters. This enables her to protect the lucrative merchandising and adaptations (for example, films and comics) arising from her novels. For more on trade mark registration see Chapter 5.2.

This also means that catchphrases or other idioms of celebrities are not formally protected in the UK by any statutory 'personality right' as there is in the US for example. The unauthorized use of a celebrity's photograph in an advertising campaign might be an infringement of the copyright in the photograph – but that copyright will be owned by the photographer, not the celebrity (unless it has been contractually assigned). The limited case law in this area points towards 'passing off' law as a remedy against 'false endorsement' or 'false attribution', but unless the incident in question is one where consumers were misled it becomes difficult to make a case stick.

Duration

For the four principal areas covered by copyright, namely musical, dramatic, literary and artistic works, the rights last for the lifetime of the author plus 70 years. This is long enough for the author's grandchildren to profit from such things as republications of a novel, or a movie adaptation. For such things as photographs, architectural plans, technical manuals and software, the same applies.

This means that the work of an author like Charles Dickens (1812–1870) is long since out of copyright, and hence adaptations of his novels into musicals, stage plays, films and television dramas can be made freely by anyone. Conversely, J R R Tolkien died in 1973, and so his works remain in copyright until 1 January 2044. Permission to adapt J R R Tolkien's *The*

Lord of the Rings into a radio play by the BBC had to be bought from whoever owned the copyright (which might have been passed on through inheritance laws or by sale), and was quite distinct from the film adaptation rights which had been sold to someone else.

For films the same formula applies – author's lifetime plus 70 years. But for a film, who is the author? Most certainly it is not any of the people in front of the camera, but rather the creative influences behind the film. For the purposes of determining the duration of the copyright, that 'author' is whichever of the following four people is the last to die: the director, the composer of the score, the author of the screenplay and the author of the script.

Copyright in radio and television broadcasts, and cable programmes, lasts for 50 years from the first transmission. For example, the BBC's copyright in the television images of the coronation of Queen Elizabeth II (1953) expired on 1 January 2004.

A typographical layout right is enjoyed by publishers, and lasts for 25 years. Even though the text in for instance a Dickens novel might be out of copyright, in choosing to arrange the words on a page in a particular font, with design choices made about margins, page breaks and illustrations, the layout of the words on the page attracts this short-lived right. Obviously this right is infringed if a photocopy is taken of the book, because such a copy captures not only the words, but also their presentation.

Other rights that have their basis in copyright law (such as semiconductor topography right and database right) were mentioned briefly in Chapter 1.3, and typically last for 15 years. Unregistered design right is discussed in more detail in Chapter 5.4.

Ownership

The creator of an original work is the first owner of its copyright. This right automatically passes to his or her employer if the work in question relates to their employment. This includes work done in the person's own time or even at home. So a software developer employed to write databases will find that his or her employer owns the copyright in the programs, whether they were produced in the office or at home. However, if that employee writes computer games in his or her spare time, he or she will retain the copyright in such games, assuming that is not part of his/her employment duties. It is worth mentioning the converse position at this point: what if the software developer pursues this hobby (writing computer games) while at work? Although the law is not definitive on this point, in several court cases the equitable solution has been for the employee to retain ownership of the copyright in the project unrelated to their work, but to be obliged to grant a free licence in the software to the employer in recognition that it was developed in the employer's time and using the employer's equipment.

The situation with regard to contractors, however, is quite different. For over 15 years the situation in the UK has been that a contractor, as the creator of the work, generally retains the legal ownership of copyright in the work unless there is a contract that is explicit to the contrary. For example, an advertising agency might be asked to develop some artwork for a client's magazine advertising campaign. It is implicit in such an arrangement that the artwork may be used in magazines. However, the contract is silent on the question of assignment of the copyright in the artwork to the client, so that copyright remains with the advertising agency. At a later date the client might take that artwork and use it in a billboard campaign, or put it on a Web site. Such uses were not implicit in the original arrangement, and the client does not have the right to copy or adapt the artwork in this fashion. The advertising agency can now demand an additional licence fee for this further use of the copyrighted material.

Many client firms are now aware of such issues, and ask about any future fees for additional uses of creative material at an early stage in the negotiations with the contractor. However, some go further and put clauses into the contracts that state that 'all copyright in this project will be assigned to us'. The client offering the contract is of course free to set out terms and conditions however it likes, but contractors should consider carefully before signing. Does the client really need the copyright in everything? For example, a contractor might be asked to propose 10 different sets of artwork for use in a promotion. Only one design is taken forward by the client, leaving nine other fledgling ideas in the bin. While the client understandably wants the copyright in the one piece of artwork that is then developed for multiple applications, does it really need the copyright in the other nine schemes it rejected? Would it not be advantageous for the copyright in the unused artwork to be retained by the contractor for development with other clients in the future? Would it not, therefore, have been more fair for the contractor to have negotiated for the contract to relate to assignment in the copyright only of the final artwork, not all artwork? This, of course, is a matter of contract law and good client relations – only those involved can decide how achievable such an approach might be.

Even after an author has exhausted the economic rights in a work (that is, has sold them all), he or she retains inalienable moral rights over how the work is used. A typical example here is a musician who assigns the copyright in his/her music to a record label, which in turn sell records and CDs and pays royalties back to the musician. Despite this, the musician retains the right to object if his/her music was used in a manner he/she dislikes (for example, in an advertisement endorsing a product to which he/she is opposed).

Such moral rights include the right to be identified as the author, or disclaimed as not the author in the event of forgeries. Such disclaimers can be seen, rarely, on movie adaptations of novels that the novelist feels has so mutilated the story that he or she wishes to be publicly dissociated from the film. Creators also have the moral right to protect their works from destruction (for example, a sculpture or mural on a building). These moral rights last as long as the copyright itself: author's lifetime plus 70 years.

Infringement

For work protected by copyright, it is an infringement for anyone to do the following without the consent of the rights owner:

- copy, reproduce or adapt (including translations);
- publicly perform (for example, pre-recorded music played in a restaurant);
- distribute, issue or rent the work;
- broadcast the work (for example, by television, radio or Internet 'Web-cast').

These are so-called 'primary infringements', and the offender is guilty whether or not they knew the material was in copyright. As is the norm in English and Scottish law, ignorance is no defence. However, for a defendant to be guilty of the 'secondary infringements' listed below, the rights owner needs to prove that the defendant knew it was dealing with infringing material:

- importing infringing material;
- selling infringing material;
- possession for business purposes (for example, pirated software on an office PC);
- facilitating infringing material (for example, providing access to a CD burner).

An example that illustrates these two types of wrongdoing is an advertising agency wilfully copying photographs it does not own and using them in artwork it supplies to a client for a brochure. The agency would be guilty of primary infringement (it should have bought permission from the photographer), and the client would be guilty of secondary infringement if it could be proved that it knew the images in the brochure belonged to someone else, but nevertheless printed and distributed the brochures.

Exceptions

The law allows for users of copyright to enjoy certain limited freedoms with regard to copyright material. For example, it is 'fair use' to photocopy a few pages from a library book as part of non-commercial research (for example, for a hobby). This of course is a world apart from a company copying whole technical journals to distribute to all its R&D staff. The line between the two is not drawn in absolute terms in the statutes, so it is pointless asking how close to the line it is safe to go in this regard. The safest course is to seek either the rights owner's permission, or seek legal advice, any time it is arguable that the copying being done is both commercial in scale and a 'substantial' taking from the original.

Newspapers often justify printing extracts from 'leaked memos' or 'private diaries' by saying that they are either reporting current affairs or exposing wrongdoing. Both memos and diaries are protected by copyright, but the two defences suggested are sometimes upheld in court. However, such matters are determined on the specific facts of each incident, and do not give rise to a strict rule applicable in all cases, which would allow the press to routinely breach copyright wherever it suited it to sensationalize a story.

Collective licensing societies

It is obvious that placing a photocopier in a library is a recipe for disaster in terms of respecting the copyright of authors and publishers! However, it is not practical to put an official next to every photocopier in such a position, so that would-be copiers can negotiate with him or her and pay for every copy they take. Rather, the practical solution is for the Copyright Licensing Authority to collect a tariff from anyone who operates a photocopier in that fashion, and distribute the revenue back to publishers and authors according to various formulae. A similar approach is taken by other 'collecting societies' like the Performing Rights Society (PRS) and Phonographic Performance Limited (PPL), which collect money from (for example) all the restaurants, hotels, nightclubs, bars and pubs that play pre-recorded music to their clientele, and from broadcasters using music in television and radio programmes. The money collected by the PRS goes back to composers, authors and publishers, whereas PPL collects on behalf of record companies. It is worth bearing in mind that buying a new music CD may come with an implicit licence to play it at home and in private, but if it is played in a shop, bar or factory, the proprietor needs to be covered by a licence from the relevant collecting society.

Evidence

To bring an infringement action, the plaintiff must be able to prove that the alleged infringer's work is a copy or adaptation of that original work. (It should be noted that if the work was not itself original it does not merit copyright protection!)

There are two common defences against an accusation of copying: first, that the accuser is in fact the infringer; and second, that the works are similar by coincidence. To counter this first defence it helps if the plaintiff can prove that the work was created before the infringer's work. Given that 'soft' rights like copyright exist without registration, there is no date stamp on an official form as there would be with a patent or trade mark. However, an *ad hoc* date stamp can be achieved by rights owners putting a copy of the work (script, software, photographs or whatever) in an envelope and sending it to themselves by registered mail. Once received it will bear a date, and can safely be stored. It should only be opened as part of court proceedings if these are required to prove whose work came first.

A certain cunning is required to beat the second defence, and it involves leaving telltale fingerprints in a work which will find their way into copies. Most commonly this is seen in the software arena, where dummy lines of code are sprinkled through a program. If it is copied, these dummy lines will be duplicated in the infringing code, and can be located by anyone who knows what to look for, although they would not be obvious to anyone else. Some court cases of infringement of software have been resolved on such simple matters as spelling mistakes in the documentation, which have been found in both the original and the copy. Web site designers can embed a shape on a Web page whose colour is coded to be 'transparent'. Anyone who 'rips' the code for that page (because he or she covets its functionality) and then tries to cover his or her tracks by changing some fonts, colours and artwork will still be caught out because the underlying code will still have the hidden shape on the page, like a watermark.

This strategy has many applications. The Ordnance Survey subtly fingerprints its maps (for example by changing the width of certain roads, or missing out an apostrophe in the name of a village). A rival using different surveyors would not have such features in its own maps. The OS specific features appeared in AA road atlases, and the damages awarded by the court amounted to £20 million, covering eight years of unpaid licence fees. A database can be littered with dummy entries, and these will be found in copies. The most obvious database for any firm to protect is its customer list. It could for example add to this list the home address of the marketing manager, with a characteristic misspelling for his or her name, or the name of the street. If any junk mail from a rival firm arrives at this address with that characteristic error in the address label, it will know that a rival has an unauthorized copy of the customer list. (Chapter 5.5 discusses what can happen when staff quit and compete against their former employer, using knowledge of the firm and its customers to their advantage.) I have done just this with all the utility companies. My house is not divided into flats, but my gas bill comes to 'Flat One', my electricity bill to 'Flat Two.'; Amazon® thinks I live in 'Flat A' and so on. If ever I get junk mail addressed to me with one of these fingerprints I simply contact the relevant company and remind it of its obligations under the Data Protection Act 1998 (Schedule 12) – and hey presto! I get a discount off my next bill.

Even though the alleged infringer's own work might enjoy a copyright of its own, that does not overcome the issue that it has its genesis in the original work. For example, someone might make a graphic novel of a stage play. The book will have a copyright of its own, even though it also infringes the copyright in the play.

Unsolicited submissions

Proving that someone else has copied a work can be hard enough, but how can any individual or organization guard against an unwarranted accusation that it has infringed copyright? In the creative industries, accusations of unscrupulous behaviour are rife, with designers investing great effort in 'pitches' to potential clients only to find that their ideas are adopted by the client, but developed by another (cheaper) contractor.

An unsolicited submission from a freelance can make life very difficult for a company, if it happens to be similar to a project on which it is already working. Now, if it completes and launch its product (perhaps an advertising campaign for a client), the freelance will recognize similarities between the product and his or her submission, and accuse the company of copying. While the coincidence is unfortunate, how can the organization guard against it? A useful bulwark is to adopt a company policy that no one from the creative team ever opens any post. All incoming mail should be handled by an administrator, whose instructions are to detect and return unsolicited creative material. A covering letter would help too. It might read, 'It is our company policy to return all unsolicited submissions. No copy of this submission has been kept. No one from our creative team has seen it.' This protocol must be proven to be sufficiently robust, and not mere lip-service, if it is to stand up in court and protect the company from accusations of cheating a freelance.

Copyright abroad

International treaties provide for reciprocal protection all over the world. For example, a foreign author's work is protected in the UK under UK copyright law as if he or she were a UK citizen, provided that the same is true for a UK author in that foreign country.

The symbol © (followed by the year and owner's name) is not always necessary, but helps the copyright owner to put others on notice that he or she knows about the rights, and tells them to whom they should apply if they need permission to copy or adapt the work. In some countries this symbol is required if the originator to invoke copyright protection laws. Some countries (for example the United States) have a Copyright Registry, but this is entirely voluntary. Deposit at the US Copyright Registry is not necessary in order for an originator to enjoy rights, but it does entitle a rights owner to additional damages in the event of infringement. Such registration puts the work on public display, meaning that many software developers are reluctant to register because they wish to retain certain trade secrets in their code. The UK abolished its Copyright Registry, which used to be held at Stationers Hall, in 1911.

For more information about any aspect of IP visit www.patent.gov.uk or call 08459 500 505.

Reddie & Grose

Do your Inventors and Designers understand what is needed from them to maximise the protection for their work?

Does your Marketing Department use your Trade Marks properly?

Does your Company suffer from a general lack of knowledge of IP rights?

Patents   Trade Marks

Designs   Copyright

Reddie & Grose is a leading UK firm of European Patent Attorneys, Chartered Patent Agents and Trade Mark Attorneys with offices in London and Cambridge. We offer a high quality service at a reasonable cost.

Our patent practitioners have particular strengths in electronics, electrical engineering, computers, communications, chemistry, biotechnology, mechanical engineering, business methods and business processes. Our trade mark attorneys practise in all fields, and we have specialists in the entertainment, communications and pharmaceutical industries.

We advise clients on the creating and management of intellectual property portfolios covering the globe. We have connections with patent and trade mark practitioners in every country.

We are happy to help in educating your staff to understand what is involved in dealing with intellectual property rights, by participating in seminars, giving talks, or preparing written guidance on Intellectual property.

If you would like more information on the services we offer, please visit our website at: www.reddie.co.uk, or telephone for a brochure or advice on 020 7242 0901.

Reddie & Grose
16 Theobalds Road
London
WC1X 8PL

Reddie & Grose
5 Shaftesbury Road
Cambridge
CB2 2BW

Designs

If your designs give you market share, says Dr Jeremy Philpott at the Patent Office, you can bet that the copycats will be in there like a shot.

In a market place crowded with similar products, how can an organization make its own stand out? A strong brand (underpinned by trade marks) is a great help, but when it is launching a new product the nascent brand lacks power. Inimitable functionality (underpinned by patents) is rarely the unique selling point of a new product. What attracts the consumer to pull the product off the shelf and into a shopping basket will be the appearance, either of the product or of its packaging. The magpie in all of us is drawn to objects because of their colour, shape and texture, regardless of whether the product has special technical features. This is where good design makes all the difference.

If an organization's design gives it market share, you can bet that the copycats will be in there like a shot. Protecting how a product is shaped or decorated through design registration is frequently ignored by many businesses, and yet this type of protection can be simpler and certainly cheaper to obtain than either patents or trade marks. To date, too many designers have assumed that copyright protects their three-dimensional articles, and hence there is no need to pay for registration. To rely on the free and automatic protection of copyright will prove to be a false economy on their part when they discover that the act of mass-producing an article means that it loses its protection under copyright law and instead must be protected under design law.

Unregistered design right

Like copyright and unregistered trade marks, this is a 'soft' right. It is easy for the right to arise, but more troublesome to enforce it. There are two dissimilar forms of unregistered design right, one based on UK law, and the other based on European Community law.

In 1988 changes to copyright law created an 'unregistered design right' for so-called 'works of utility', for example those articles subject to mass manufacture and lacking artistic merit in their own right. Examples include door handles, shower trays and plastic coats. This right extends to such things as internal configurations where the shape is critical to the article, but not apparent to the naked eye (for example the interior of a carburettor).

The right lasts for only 10 years from first marketing of the article, or 15 years from first design, whichever is the shorter. Just as with copyright, the right cannot be enforced if the originator cannot prove copying. What is more, in the last five years of the right's existence, the owner is powerless to prevent copying if he or she is paid a licence fee (that is, a royalty) by a third party. This is a so-called 'licence of right', and it permits others to approach the design right owner and offer a fee in exchange for permission to copy the design. The owner cannot refuse, although he or she can argue over the price for the licence. If such negotiations do not result in an agreement, the parties can come to the Patent Office where a royalty rate will be imposed.

The EC unregistered design right has only been around since 2002, and has several important differences from the UK system. While it is an automatic 'soft' right, it lasts only three years from the first public disclosure of the design. What is more, to be deserving of this brief free protection the design must meet all the criteria that apply to designs seeking to be worthy of registration. Crucially, among these is the stipulation that only outward appearance is protected by design registration, so by implication internal configurations are not protected by this right across the EU, in the same way that UK unregistered design right affords protection.

Registered designs

Long regarded as the poor relation in intellectual property, design registration is now enjoying a renaissance thanks to recent changes to the law. Protection for designs is now more potent and more flexible than ever before.

The UK signed on to the European Directive on Design Registration at the end of 2001, and this has broadened the range of products or designs that can be protected, and increased the scope of that protection. Such things as digitized icons (see Figure 5.4.1) and computer-generated characters can now be registered, so if, for example, games software is copied, the creator could bring an action under design law (for the way things look on the screen), which might give more immediate results than an accusation of copyright infringement ('piracy') of the underlying code. Remember, to bring an action under copyright law the plaintiff must prove copying or adaptation from the original work. The defendant can get off the hook if he or she convinces the court that his or her work is the same merely by coincidence. This is not so in design law – if a rival product or design looks the same as the originally registered one, copy or fluke, the originator can stop its production.

Under the old law, anyone wanting to protect a graphic design across a range of products (which might include clothing, crockery or souvenirs) would have needed separate registrations for each article, and had no remedy against the design appearing on different types of articles from those registered (such as calendars and magazines). Now it is the design itself that is protected, irrespective of where it appears. This means that such things as logos can now be registered as designs. In rebranding itself, Arsenal Football Club has exploited this change in the law to best effect. Its old logo is only a registered trade mark and it had a lengthy tussle with a small trader, Mr Reed, over his selling of 'unofficial' scarves, hats and shirts bearing the Arsenal name and cannon motif. Much of the legal argument turned on whether consumers bought Mr Reed's goods because they were confused about their origin (a trade mark abuse) or simply to show their club loyalty (argued to be a defence). However, Arsenal's new logo is not only a registered trade mark, but also a registered design. With the registered design there is no need to argue issues of confusion to customers or harm to trade – any copying of the new logo can be halted on the simple basis that this logo is the exclusive property of the Arsenal FC, and any designs that a court considers to look similar can be seized.

The new Arsenal logo also illustrates a new requirement in design law: that to deserve protection a design must not only be novel, but must also have 'individual character' – it must be sufficiently distinct from other designs already known to the public. In comparing the new and old Arsenal logos it is clear that they have moved as far away from the old design as possible, while retaining the essential elements of the name and cannon. This criterion means that simply copying another design and making some minor modifications to it will not be enough to entitle the producer to a

Figure 5.4.1 Digitalized icons for display on electronic equipment, registered as designs by Vodafone Group plc *and reproduced with their kind permission.*

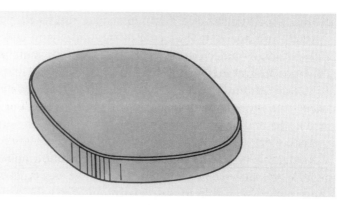

Figure 5.4.2 Pfizer's patents on Viagra's active ingredient, sildenafil, will eventually expire. Their name, and that of the product will remain as registered trade marks, outliving their patents. But, in addition, Pfizer have a registered design on how their tablet appears: no-one else may make a blue diamond-shaped table exactly like this during the term of the right. *The design registration is reproduced with the kind permission of Pfizer inc.*

design registration. Furthermore, if the design it mimicked was itself registered, the similar design could be viewed by a court as an infringement and land it in trouble!

Although design registration is cheap (just £60 for the first 5 years, renewable for up to 25 years), many designers make large numbers of new creations every year, and it had been difficult for them to know which ones to register. The introduction of a 12-month 'grace period' now

Figure 5.4.3 Arsenal's logos, both old (left) and new (right). Though both are registered trade marks, only the new one is also registered as a design, having 'individual character' over its predecessor. *Reproduced with the kind permission of Arsenal Football Club.*

makes life much easier for them. Designers can now put products on the market – perhaps a range of 20 different tiles – and having seen which ones sell best (maybe just three in the range), acquire registrations only for the ones that matter to them and their market. Their registration must be made within a year of their first public disclosure of the design, otherwise the application will be invalid for 'lack of novelty', and if registered will be unenforceable.

Since April 2003 it has been possible to register designs at the European Community level at the Office for Harmonization in the Internal Market (OHIM) in Alicante. As mentioned in Chapter 5.2 (with regard to EC trade marks), OHIM is able to register a single right that is binding in all EU member states. This can make for a very cost-effective one-stop shop for a registration to cover 25 European countries.

For more information about any aspect of IP visit www.patent.gov.uk or call 08459 500 505.

Know-how, trade secrets and confidentiality

Sensitive information can easily end up in the wrong hands. Are there any steps you can take to protect yourself? asks Dr Jeremy Philpott of the Patent Office.

Any business continually risks leaks of valuable information. Its staff will have know-how that makes its processes optimal. This know-how is like the difference between having a robot bake a cake and having a master chef do the job. Business consultants and venture partners also know the company's weaknesses, and next month might be working with its competitors. The marketing team are paid to boast about what the products can do. The organization should not ever let them know what its R&D team is developing, or they might blab to all its customers! Even suppliers might engage in idle gossip with their other customers (the firm's competitors) about the unusual raw materials it has recently ordered for a new project.

The other rights discussed in Part 5 of the book all have a statutory basis, but it is not so with the rights covered here. There is no 'Confidence and Trade Secrets Act 1981' or the like. However, the principles discussed below have evolved in the common law through pragmatic court rulings over the last 150 years.

Confidence

The law has shown that an obligation of confidence can arise even without a contractual obligation. Both doctors and solicitors owe their patients and clients a duty of confidence without any formal agreement being signed. When an organization deals with third parties like investors, consultants and product developers, a confidentiality agreement (or non-disclosure agreement) helps put that obligation on a contractual basis. (It is often preferable, in the event of a leak, to sue for breach of contract rather than for breach of confidence.) However, such written agreements are not magic talismans, and their widespread use must be tempered. Just as confidentiality can arise even without a written agreement (as with a doctor/patient relationship), it can also not be present *despite* a written agreement.

Information that is already in the public domain cannot be made the subject of a confidentiality agreement. This much is obvious. If the ingredients for a curry sauce are written on the side of the bottle in the shops, the producer cannot prevent its staff from disclosing what the ingredients are. (Whether they are allowed to disclose the precise ratios, or special treatments of the ingredients, is another matter.) But in numerous precedents the courts have come to the view that the information loses its essential quality of confidence when the first owner of that information *loses control over how it is distributed.* So despite being labelled 'confidential' a document will be treated as public domain if it is left lying around an office, posted on the Internet or circulated outside the firm. Similarly, if a business obliges one party to sign a confidentiality agreement with respect to some information, and then freely discloses it to others, the first party will no longer be bound by the agreement. And having each of 50 different people sign separate confidentiality agreements with regard to the same secret is unlikely to impress to a court – can the organization honestly say it has kept control over what every one of those 50 people might disclose?

Restrictive covenants

In a case reported in the press as the 'Frozen chicken wars', a company that regularly delivered poultry to local caterers lost business to a new delivery firm set up by a former employee, the aptly named Mr Fowler. The company, Faccenda Chicken Ltd (FCL), discovered that the Mr Fowler was supplying chickens to the same customers as FCL supplied, just before FCL's own delivery times. FCL sued for breach of confidence, given that Mr Fowler was seemingly taking advantage of his 'inside knowledge' of FCL's customer list and delivery schedules. Because of the specific facts of the case the court felt that there was nothing uniquely special in, first, knowing to whom to sell chickens, and for how much, and second, knowing when to deliver them, which endowed that information with the essential qualities of confidence. A prosecution for breach of fidelity (an employee's implicit duty to be faithful to his or her employer) would not have worked either because the rival firm was staffed by former, not current, employees.

A possible defence against such disloyalty is a 'restrictive covenant' in the terms of an employment contract. The covenant forbids employees from doing certain things within a specified period and/or area after leaving an employer. For example, FCL's employment contracts could have said, 'You may not work in the chicken delivery trade within five miles of our depot within six months of leaving our firm.' However, restrictive covenants are not permitted to be used simply to prevent competition from former employees. Courts will only enforce them where staff are seeking to exploit information specific to their former employer, such as knowledge of internal processes, pricing strategies, marketing campaigns or carefully cultivated client relations.

Such clauses in employment contracts must be very modest in their limitations. If a court feels that a restriction is too onerous the entire clause will be struck out, and it cannot be reduced in scope after the event. This means that a restrictive covenant preventing a plumber from working within 50 miles of his former employer would be unreasonable, because such work is highly localized, and the skills of one plumber are very much like those of dozens of others in the same town. Similarly, a software engineer's restrictive covenant would be unenforceable if she was prevented from using her skills for a period of five years after leaving a particular employer, because such technology changes rapidly. The specialist aspects of her skill-set on leaving a firm would probably be obsolete in less than a year, so there would be no need to restrict her for any longer than that.

At all times it is important to differentiate between information well known in the relevant trade, and information unique to a specific employer. The former kind of information, such as how to weld copper pipes, could never be the subject of a confidentiality agreement or a restrictive covenant. The latter, for example one firm's uniquely developed solder or tool for use in welding copper pipes, could be a trade secret and worthy of a restrictive covenant.

Know-how and trade secrets

Several sections of this book discuss patents in detail. The word itself means 'open' or in plain view. Patents are the antithesis of a trade secret because all the details of how an invention works are published for everyone to look at. For an invention that is a product, trade secrecy is simply not possible. Once the organization sells the product its customers and competitors can pull it apart and determine how to copy it. In these circumstances only patents, or possibly design rights, offer a remedy for copying.

But what if the new invention is a process? Perhaps the organization has developed a cheaper way to produce conventional goods, but the products themselves give no clue that they were produced by a more efficient process. In this circumstance it may decide to keep the process a trade secret, because publication of the process details in a patent would inspire its competitors to seek out alternative process improvements. This decision must be made with care, because trade secrets come with two distinct risks. First, once the secret is leaked the organization can never get it back. Sure, it can sue the employee or spy who leaked the secret, but that will not prevent other rivals from benefiting from what is now in the public domain. The second risk is that a rival might develop the same process at a later date, and obtain a patent for it. Its patent will be valid, because the 'secret' process is not in the public domain and so is not a novelty-destroying prior disclosure with respect to the patent.

A compromise between full disclosure in a patent and trade secrecy is to publish a patent application whose disclosure is 'sufficient' while still holding back an additional complementary piece of information. This extra cherry is the 'know-how'. For example, a new product is made in a chemical process performed at high temperature and pressure. The patent for the novel process would disclose that yields of 80 per cent are possible if the process is performed at between 550–750 °C and 7–9 atmospheres. However, only the patentees know that to get a yield of 98 per cent the reaction must be done at 690 °C and 7.24 atmospheres. Such a strategy comes with two caveats. First, the patent applicant must not withhold an essential piece of information. For example, if the chemical process described above will not work at the relevant temperatures and pressures without the presence of a special catalyst, and the applicant does not disclose that fact, the patent application will be invalid because its disclosure is 'insufficient' to allow others to repeat the invention. Second, note that in the United States there is an obligation on patent applicants to disclose the 'best mode' of carrying out an invention – so if the applicant knows the optimal conditions for that 98 per cent yield it must describe them.

If the organization can stay the right side of these caveats, know-how can become a valuable business asset in its own right. An infringer of a patent might be more inclined to buy a licence if the patentee is also offering it know-how. When licensing inventions, the organization should wrap up the patent with the know-how and call it a 'technology licence,' so that even if the patent expires the licensee is still tied in by virtue of the know-how it continues to employ.

For more information about any aspect of IP visit www.patent.gov.uk or call 08459 500 505.

6
Enforcing rights

What protection to expect

Before resorting to legal action against infringers, remember IP rights give you a good deal of effective protection, says Alan Wilson at Barker Brettell.

Scope of protection

For all types of IP rights, the extent of protection that can be obtained is closely related to the extent to which the product, or the name it is proposed to market it under, is different from other products or names. The scope of patent claims will depend on how novel the product is. The scope of a registered design will depend on how original the design is. The scope of trade mark rights depends on how distinctive the trade mark is. However, having good broad protection is only useful if it can be enforced in some way against others who might wish to benefit from the originator's investment by using the design, technology or the originator's reputation.

Methods of enforcement

The main way in which organizations and individuals might expect to enforce their IP rights is by taking legal action against any infringers. This can of course be very effective, and it will be necessary in some cases to stop infringement of rights. However, legal proceedings involve a considerable amount of time and resources. It is therefore worth remembering that IP rights can provide a good deal of effective protection without the necessity of resorting to legal action. There are a number of steps that can be taken to ensure that originators and owners of IP get the protection they deserve.

Product marking

Many people are largely unaware of IP rights, and tend to assume that if they see a good idea in the market place they can copy it. Marking products to indicate that they involve IP rights discourages this type of activity. The essential thing is to use marking that clearly identifies the rights that are being invoked, and to keep it up to date. There are two good reasons for this. First, people will be more likely to take notice of rights that are clearly identified, and second, it is, in some cases, an offence to claim to have IP rights that you do not in fact have.

For many types of IP there is a recognized method of marking products to alert others to the existence of rights. For example they could be marked:

- patented: GB 2012345 – to indicate that they are covered by a granted patent;
- patent pending: GB 2012345 – to indicate that there is a pending patent application;
- ©2004 ABC plc – to indicate that the products are covered by copyright;
- ® after the trade mark – to indicate that it is registered;
- ™ after the trade mark, to indicate that the user considers it to be distinctive of their goods or services and wishes to prevent others from using it, for example under the laws of passing off.

Of course it will never be clear exactly what effect these markings have, because people will not come and tell the originator that they have decided not to copy the ideas. However, it is a fact that many people make their first contact with patent and trade mark attorneys with the question, 'I want to copy this product, but it is marked with the following. Please can you advise me whether this means anything?' Usually the advice is that it does.

Take prompt action

If the organization becomes aware that somebody might be infringing its IP rights, it is important to take action sooner rather than later. Sometimes it might be tempting to delay, either because it is hoped the infringement might stop without any need to take action, or because the IP owner wants the damage to build up so that it can 'sue the infringer for lots of money'. However, delay can seriously affect the ability to enforce the rights.

In the extreme, if the complainant delays long enough, the legal defences of 'laches' and 'estoppel' might be invoked by the infringer. The effect of these is that, if the complainant has delayed so long that the infringer thinks that it (or he/she) does not intend to take any action, the infringer can assume that the rights owner has no objection to its activities. The infringer might then be allowed to continue when attempts are finally made to stop it. However, these defences are quite rare. More important in many cases is the advantage of the organization having a reputation for enforcing its rights. If one of its competitors is seen to infringe its rights and 'get away with it', others will soon assume that it either cannot, or does not want to, enforce its rights. Once infringement has become widespread, it can be much harder to stop it than if it had been 'nipped in the bud'.

The first steps of enforcement

When the organization (or individual) first becomes aware that somebody is infringing its IP rights, its first steps will probably depend on who the alleged infringer is; what relationship, if any, the organization has with it; and the infringer's relative strengths and weaknesses compared with the organization's. Relevant questions to ask include:

- Is the infringer likely to respond to reasonable negotiation?
- Is the aim to stop the infringer's actions altogether, or extract money from it in return for allowing it to continue?
- Could the organization afford legal action if it became necessary to achieve its aims?
- Could the infringer afford legal action if the organization started it?

Another important question is, how strong is the IP protection? For example, some patents cover inventions that are so different from anything that is previously known that the patentee can be reasonably confident that they will be upheld by a court if challenged. Other patents cover minor improvements over the prior art, such that a court might disagree with the patent office that granted the patent, and find that the invention lacks sufficient inventive step, and is therefore invalid. It is of course best to seek advice on this if the organization is considering enforcing its rights.

Clearly these and other factors will determine the manner in which to approach the alleged infringer. This can vary between a conciliatory approach, in which it is suggested that the infringer might like to pay a reasonable royalty to continue with its activities, to a more aggressive approach in which the complainant makes its position clear, sets reasonable deadlines for response, and indicates that it will start legal proceedings if the response is not satisfactory.

Unjustified threats of infringement proceedings

One factor to bear in mind is that for some forms of IP rights, in particular patents and registered designs, it is unlawful to make unjustified threats of infringement proceedings against those who are not the original producers or importers of the infringing articles. The reason for this is to prevent bullying tactics against customers who might be persuaded to change supplier to avoid any possibility of an IP dispute, regardless of the validity of the claim against them. In view of these threats provisions it is important, when approaching an alleged infringer, to make sure they are not unintentionally given grounds to sue on the basis of unjustified threats.

Remedies the court can provide for infringement

Legal proceedings will generally take up a lot of time and resources. However, if the complaintant does proceed with legal action against an infringer of its rights, and is successful at the end of the trial, which will generally take several months at least, the main remedies it can obtain can be very effective. They often include damages to compensate it for the effects of the infringing activity, for example any profits it has lost as a result of the infringement, and an injunction to prevent further infringement.

If the business is particularly seriously threatened by the infringing activities, and it clearly has a strong case, it might even be able to obtain an 'interim injunction' within a matter of weeks, preventing the activities of the infringer until the full trial has been conducted. In this circumstance it is usual to need to set money aside to compensate the other party for loss of business in the event that the legal challenge fails.

Alan Wilson is a partner at Barker Brettell, mainly involved in patent drafting and prosecution work. He is a chartered physicist with experience in the fields of telecoms, computing and medical physics. For further information please contact Alan Wilson, Barker Brettell, 138 Hagley Road, Edgbaston, Birmingham B16 9PW; tel: +44 (0)121 456 1364; fax: +44 (0)121 456 1368; URL: www.barkerbrettell.co.uk; e-mail: alan.wilson@barkerbrettell.co.uk

Design protection

There are eight lines of defence for your designs, says Geoffrey Adams at the British Copyright Council.

All managers and designers should be aware of the opportunities offered by national and international systems of protection, so that full advantage can be made of them – and, where necessary, action taken to avoid the pitfalls. Company policies towards design protection should be clear, unequivocal in their principles, and carried out consistently. They should involve the following.

1 Recognition of the value of design protection

No industry – or designer – will happily accept the flagrant copying of its work and the resulting damage to profitability. Few can rely on keeping processes secret from competitors, nor on such a rapid turnover of ideas that it will keep them permanently ahead of the field. Even if that were possible, the result of constant change would inevitably be that none of the designs could be fully exploited for quantity production.

In addition, the economic value of some patents, trade marks and designs is such that failure to extract the maximum return from ownership rights would make no sense commercially. A basic appreciation of the importance of design protection should be recognized as an integral part of the management function.

2 Action to avoid endangering protection

It is essential that everything necessary is done during the design process to ensure that protection is not endangered. In addition to fulfilling the basic criteria of the relevant form of protection – from the stringent demands of patents to the originality requirement for copyright – this includes full record keeping (particularly as regards changes in ownership of rights) and attention to details of packaging, labelling and marking.

Ideally, potential problems should be spotted before they arise, especially where possible infringements (by the company or a competitor) are concerned. Senior management must be alerted to serious instances and remedial action – probably including specialist advice – should be taken. Checks need to be made against existing registers to ensure that there is no danger of 'innocent infringement'.

3 Avoiding infringements

There will always be the temptation to take advantage of demonstrably successful designs. Designing around patents and registered designs might be a legitimate pursuit, but it must be a cardinal principle not to infringe the rights of others. There will inevitably be areas of uncertainty, where dividing lines cannot be clearly drawn. In many cases independent designs may flow from the same source of inspiration.

There is also the complication of 'commonplace' designs (as in the UK design right) for which no protection is available. But a respect for the principle of avoiding infringements is important for the medium and long-term standing of an enterprise.

4 Deterring infringements

All staff, especially sales staff, should be alert to spotting infringements of the company's designs. Early knowledge can save a great deal of damage and expense. A company policy to pursue infringements, supported by a reputation for taking action, will itself act as a powerful deterrent to would-be plagiarists. Action might not even be necessary: evidence of determination alone may be sufficient to discourage or to stop infringers. Publicity, particularly in the trade press, may have a useful role to play in establishing such an image.

5 Making a commercial judgement

If action does prove necessary, the decision whether or not to proceed must be a commercial one. Factors to be taken into account include the costs involved (staff time as well as legal advice), the comparative financial strength of the parties, and a realistic assessment of the damage done by the infringing product in the market place. Bearing in mind that, even in a successful action, the costs are unlikely to be fully recovered, it might be wiser to reach an out-of-court settlement (perhaps involving the grant of a licence, on carefully defined terms, to the competing manufacturer).

6   Alternatives to court action

Before resorting to the courts, careful consideration should be given to alternative means of resolving disputes. A number of professional bodies and trade associations in the UK have developed codes of practice, binding on their members, relating to intellectual property issues in design. Some go further in providing the means of resolving disputes between members or, where both parties are prepared to accept the association's decision, between a member and an outside complainant.

This has proved particularly successful in industries where copying has often been endemic, or in situations where economic considerations make recourse to the courts unviable. Examples are the carpet, fashion and furniture industries. In no case is resort to the law prevented, but it might well be more attractive to both parties to resolve matters more speedily, less expensively and perhaps without the publicity attendant on a court hearing.

The Patent Office has the power under UK law to resolve a number of patent, design and trade mark issues that are in dispute (including arbitration over the terms of licences of right).

7   Obtaining an injunction

Where infringement is suspected, prompt action is essential. A formal complaint might be sufficient to secure withdrawal of the offending product, particularly where the infringement has resulted from genuine ignorance. However, care should be taken before threatening legal proceedings in disputes relating to design rights, since threats that prove 'groundless' might themselves be the subject of legal proceedings against the person making them. (This also applies in the patent and trade mark, though not copyright, fields.)

If a formal complaint is unsuccessful, it may be possible to obtain an injunction to halt the infringement pending a full trial of the case. This might be enough to end the court proceedings, since a defendant may well decide that it is not worthwhile to continue fighting the case, especially taking the likely cost into account.

8   Court actions

In the UK, the full range of civil courts is available for the resolution of disputes deemed to be serious enough to require this approach. Cases may be heard in the High Court or, for smaller, less complex issues, in the Patents County Court, before specially appointed judges experienced in trying such matters. There is the possibility of appealing decisions to the Court of Appeal and, ultimately, to the House of Lords.

Although industrial property and copyright disputes will normally take the form of civil cases, penal sanctions may be available. The provisions of the UK law in this respect have been strengthened in recent years, particularly to counter flagrant, or repeated, breaches of the law.

Geoffrey Adams is an adviser in design protection law and practice. He is also is an honorary fellow of the Chartered Society of Designers and is Vice-President of the British Copyright Council. Tel: 020 7226 7364.

IP theft

The theft of intellectual property is not yet equated in the public mind with other offences against property, such as fraud, theft and trespass, says Michael Blakeney, Director of the Queen Mary Intellectual Property Research Institute at the University of London.

The terms 'counterfeiting' and 'piracy' in relation to goods refer to the manufacture, distribution and sale of copies of goods that have been made without the authority of the owner of the intellectual property. These goods are intended to appear to be so similar to the original as to be passed off as genuine items. This includes the use of famous brands on pharmaceutical products, clothing, perfumes and household products not manufactured by or on behalf of the owner of the trade mark, as well as exact copies of CDs containing music or software, which are traded in a form intended to be indistinguishable to ordinary consumers from the genuine product.

In a criminal law context, intellectual property counterfeiting and piracy are defined as contraband activities that centre on the illegal production and sale of goods that are intended to pass for the real product. In this context 'contraband' is goods whose importation, exportation or possession is forbidden. Dealings in contraband invariably involve smuggling, where the manufacturers and distributors of these products also seek to evade taxes on the production and wholesaling of these products.

Causes of piracy and counterfeiting

The principal cause of piracy and counterfeiting is the incentive to unscrupulous traders of the considerable business profits that can be made from free-riding on the creative efforts and investment of others, by passing off imitations of desired products at a lower cost than those that are incurred by the producers of genuine products. Obviously, this trade would not exist without consumer demand and the public perception that piracy and counterfeiting are innocuous infractions. The theft of intellectual property is not yet equated in the public mind with other offences against property: crimes such as fraud, theft and trespass. This is exacerbated by, one, a failure by public authorities and commercial organizations to communicate to the consuming public the dangers from the use of unauthorized products, and the deleterious social welfare effects from this trade; and two, the imposition of inadequately deterrent penalties by the judicial authorities.

The World Customs Organization observes that the evolution of many contraband markets is typically a progression through one or more of the following stages:

- grey market, or parallel, trading;
- smuggling;
- counterfeiting and piracy.

Thus some markets, like those for contraband cigarettes, alcohol and pharmaceuticals, evolve through all three stages. Others – like the contraband markets for branded apparel and software – might move directly from grey market trading to counterfeiting.

In Western Europe and North America, the easiest way to meet consumer demand for a cheaper product is through so-called grey market, or parallel, trading. Grey market goods are sold outside established distribution agreements, and their purveyors take advantage of the fact that companies charge different prices for their products in different markets.

In a number of jurisdictions, strong links have been noted between the grey market and smuggling, and in a number of sectors grey market channels have been used to camouflage counterfeit products. In the fashion, sportswear and software sectors, it is not uncommon in the grey market for traders to send genuine samples to the importer and mix the consignment with counterfeits.

In markets for high-tax products, such as tobacco and alcohol, where grey market products might not be available, smuggling becomes the primary means of meeting the demand for those products. In smuggling, organized crime groups establish elaborate means of concealing their diversion of products from the legal to the illegal market. This is to avoid law enforcement initiatives and those by private industries seeking to maintain the integrity of their supply chains. The smuggling techniques are complex and transnational in scope, and might involve complex transactions with the involvement of legitimate as well as illicit enterprises. The objective is to make smuggling routes and the structure of transactions as complicated as possible, with the largest possible range of owners in a very short space of time, in order to make police and customs investigations as difficult as possible. The primary objective is to make the final owner untraceable and to make the links between the successive owners as ambiguous as possible.

In some cases grey market goods are not available, and organized crime groups might decide to ensure a steady source of supply by becoming vertically integrated for the purposes of producing and distributing counterfeit and pirate products. This involves developing a supply chain that is wholly in the hands of organized crime groups, from rogue manufacturing through to smuggling the contraband across international borders, to illegal distribution and retailing to consumers.

The development of digitization and the availability of used manufacturing equipment have facilitated the counterfeiting and piracy of a variety of products, from traditional industries like cigarettes and apparel to high-tech sectors like computer software and music CDs.

- Rogue manufacturing sectors, which produce counterfeit and pirated products, have much, much lower production costs:
- They are usually located in developing nations with extremely low labour and material costs.
- The quality of material inputs is extremely low.
- Quality control is virtually non-existent and the production facilities are often dirty, squalid workshops.
- They are virtually cash businesses. Payment is received either in cash, or within 8 to 10 days of a shipment being delivered. There is little need to finance receivables on a long-term basis.
- There is little, if any, inventory. Production is closely tied to orders. This reduces the need to finance inventories and makes detection very difficult.
- There are no costs associated with the oversight and accountability under which lawful businesses operate.

Impacts of counterfeiting and piracy

The costs to those businesses whose products are pirated and counterfeited include:

- loss of sales;
- competitive disadvantage against those enterprises that free-ride on the research and development and marketing expenses of legitimate enterprises;

- the possibility of product liability from defective imitation products;
- loss of goodwill and prestige by a brand, where counterfeits are freely available;
- the expense of monitoring the market and instituting legal proceedings against infringers.

These costs will be incurred in both developed and developing countries. The losses sustained by industry will be reflected in losses to the public revenue, as well as in unemployment in the affected industries.

The prevalence of infringing activities in a country will also discourage investment from those industries in which proprietary rights are important. Thus, for example, the pirating of music CDs and computer software will discourage investment in the music and information technology sectors.

As counterfeiting and piracy are illicit activities, they will be engaged in by criminals, who will use their gains from these activities to subsidize further criminal activities. As these activities are not engaged in by ethical businesses, the businesses will not observe basic employment standards, will avoid contributing to public revenues through the payment of taxes and excise, and have no concern that the products they produce are of an acceptable consumer standard.

All countries, whether developed, developing or least developed, are vulnerable to trade diversion from piracy and counterfeiting. For example, the development of extensive computer software and movie industries in India has spawned equally extensive developments in copyright piracy affecting those industries. The global market for folkloric works, including music, art, sculptures, textile products and other artefacts, has spawned a global industry for the counterfeiting of these products. With the development of niche markets for agricultural products, an illicit market has developed in which geographical indications are counterfeited.

The tax and excise losses caused by counterfeiting and piracy are considerable. As this trade tends to be clandestine, the producers of infringing products will also hide the size of their production output from the tax authorities. False documentation will accompany the false products, understating their sale price, for the purpose of reducing tax imposts in both the producing and importing countries.

The major cost to those developing countries in which piracy and counterfeiting occur is the loss of access to foreign investment, because of concerns by investors that intellectual property that is produced as the result of the relevant investment will be stolen by others. Similarly, technology transfer arrangements will be difficult to secure, where the basis of those arrangements is the bundling of proprietary technologies as part of the technology package. If there is an ineffective legal regime for the protection of those technologies, their transfer will be discouraged. In social terms, the damage suffered by businesses because of counterfeiting and piracy is reflected ultimately in their impact upon employment.

Counterfeiting and piracy have an adverse effect upon public security, where profits from such trade are appropriated by organized crime, which uses them as a means of recycling and laundering the proceeds of other unlawful activities (arms trading, drug dealing and so on). Counterfeiting and piracy, which were once craft activities, have become almost industrial-scale activities offering criminals the prospect of large economic profit without excessive risk. Their scale is now beginning to exceed that of drugs and arms dealing, on a profit/weight basis. The World Economic Forum in Davos in January 2003 was informed by the World Customs Organization (WCO) that the trade in counterfeit and pirate products was as high as US $450 billion per annum, was controlled by organized crime and was being used to fund terrorist activity.

Professor Michael Blakeney is Herchel Smith Professor of Intellectual Property Law at Queen Mary, University of London and Director of the Queen Mary Intellectual Property Research Institute, which is a part of the Centre for Commercial Law Studies (CCLS) at Queen Mary, University of London. CCLS is the focal point in the UK for teaching and research in commercial law, a field in which it enjoys an international reputation. It is also a forum for testing new ideas and exchanging information, views and expertise among academics, practitioners and those engaged in finance, commerce and industry. For further information: tel: +44 (0)20 7882 5718; e-mail: m.blakeney@qmul.ac.uk www.qmipri.org

Counterfeiting

Counterfeit goods could account for as much as 7 per cent of world trade. Steven Matz at the ICC Counterfeiting Intelligence Bureau reports on ways to prevent loss of sales and dilution of a brand.

It is often said that 'if you can make it, they can fake it', and there have been plenty of examples in recent years that show the diversity of products being counterfeited. This includes those goods most people think of when counterfeiting is mentioned, such as designer clothing, music CDs, films, software, perfume and handbags, but also other everyday items like cigarettes and spirits, and more unusual items, for example council refuse bags. The list is endless and ever-growing. For as long as the marginal revenue of a product exceeds its marginal costs, counterfeiters will be attracted to enter the market.

For goods such as clothing and digital media, the counterfeiter will readily find a willing market among a large slice of the population whose desire for the latest fashion item, album, film or piece of software outweighs their scruples.

Consumers might also be duped into buying a counterfeit product because the packaging and outward appearance of the item are such that they find it difficult to tell it apart from the genuine product. This has become an increasing problem with the use of modern technology by counterfeiters, enabling better copies to be made of both the product and packaging, and is particularly worrying where the counterfeit products pose a health risk. For example, in the UK there have been a number of instances of counterfeit spirits (vodka and whisky) containing very dangerous levels of methanol, and counterfeit cigarettes that are not only made with poor-quality tobacco but also have much higher nicotine and tar levels than genuine cigarettes.

The ICC Counterfeiting Intelligence Bureau (CIB) estimates that counterfeiting accounts for 5–7 per cent of world trade. However, precise figures are difficult to obtain, not least because of the clandestine nature of counterfeiting. To a company, though, the most important piece of data is whether any of it's products are being counterfeited and in what quantity, and what it can do about it.

For a company whose products are being counterfeited the most obvious effect is a loss of sales, but another repercussion is the dilution of the brand, especially with designer labels and luxury goods. There might also be a loss of goodwill, if a consumer who unwittingly buys a counterfeit thinking it to be genuine blames the legitimate manufacturer for a poor-quality product. Sometimes it is through such complaints by consumers that the brand owner (or right holder) discovers that there is a counterfeiting problem. Seizures by customs and law enforcement, and test purchases, are some of the other ways in which companies can become aware that their products are being counterfeited or whether a continuing problem is getting worse.

One of the steps that companies can take to reduce the level of counterfeiting is the use of anti-counterfeiting technologies on the product or packaging, or both. The use of such devices, of which there is a vast range to choose from, makes the task of producing a sophisticated counterfeit that much harder and more expensive, and can lead to the counterfeiter choosing a similar but less well-protected product. Effective overt (visible to the naked eye) anti-counterfeiting technologies enable the consumer to recognize, avoid and hopefully report instances of counterfeiting, whereas covert technologies (undetectable without special equipment) will alert company representatives and law enforcement authorities to counterfeiting activity. Anti-counterfeiting technologies can also provide vital evidential support should the need arise. Each year, the CIB publishes a directory containing details of major players in the anti-counterfeiting technology field, which can be downloaded free by visiting the CIB section of the ICC Web site at www.icc-ccs.org.

Monitoring the sale and distribution of counterfeit products across towns, cities and countries, and in markets, shops, wholesalers and factories, can be expensive. This can be a particular problem for smaller companies which lack the resources of large corporations to wage a sustained anti-counterfeiting campaign. However, one way around this is a strategy that in effect uses members of the public as unpaid investigators, providing intelligence on the source and the scale of any counterfeiting. This is a strategy that has been used in the past very successfully. In essence it involves incorporating covert anti-counterfeiting technologies into promotional material or in the packaging, for example registration forms or coupons that consumers are encouraged to return by the offer of an incentive such as a free gift or a discount on a future purchase. As the counterfeiter will usually try to mimic the entirety of the packaging, the promotional offers to consumers are also likely to be copied.

However, the use of covert anti-counterfeiting technologies will allow the brand owner/right holder to easily spot any copies. Thus, if the company receives, for example, fake coupons or registration forms, a picture can be built up of the location, source and prevalence of the counterfeit products.

In many cases, the counterfeit products will have been manufactured abroad, for example China, making it difficult, time-consuming and expensive for a variety of reasons to shut down the source. Where the sale of counterfeit goods takes place in the company's own country, or one with strong IP laws, an effective strategy is to concentrate efforts on discovering the identity of the importer(s) and taking appropriate legal action to make it financially unviable for them to continue to deal in the counterfeits.

Stopping counterfeit goods before they have a chance to enter the country from outside the EU has a better chance of success if the company lodges an IPR application with Customs. The administration fee for doing so was abolished in the UK in October 2003 and elsewhere in the EU in July 2004. Once accepted, Customs can detain goods suspected of being counterfeit for up to 10 days, which run from the time the brand owner/right holder is notified of the detention of the goods. This is subject to the company giving an undertaking to indemnify Customs against any liability or expenses that might result from the detention.

It is helpful if companies provide Customs with a detailed description of products they wish to be covered by the application, to aid Customs in distinguishing infringing goods. If there has been a previous counterfeiting problem and there are known differences or mistakes on the packaging or product, for example spelling errors or incorrect batch numbers, or there is other intelligence such as suspected suppliers of counterfeit goods or expected supply routes of suspected goods, these details should also be given. Customs should also be provided with details of who should be contacted in the event that goods suspected of being counterfeit are detained, so the goods can be inspected and confirmation given whether or not they are counterfeit. An out-of-office-hours telephone number at which the contact person can be reached might also prove useful. Customs can also act on its own initiative to detain goods suspected of being counterfeit for up to three days under a procedure called an ex-officio action. This allows a brand owner/right holder that has not lodged an application time to do so. (For further information please see: www.hmce.gov.uk/forms/notices/34.htm).

Counterfeit goods, especially clothing and luxury goods such as handbags and watches, are also being increasingly sold through the Internet, with the Web sites often run from overseas locations. An immediate and usually effective response is to contact the host ISP to shut down the infringing site. However, sites that have been removed have a habit of reappearing, so locating infringing sites is an ongoing task. Given the myriad of Web sites that exist on the Internet, finding all infringing sites using a standard search engine is nigh on impossible. Where the problem justifies the expense, the use of a bespoke search engine tailored for this purpose should be considered.

The suggestions outlined above are by no means exhaustive, nor do they discuss the application of traditional legal remedies such as search and seizure orders, which are covered elsewhere in this publication, but hopefully they will give companies affected by counterfeiting some ideas in adopting an overall anti-counterfeiting strategy. The CIB is always pleased to advise companies in such matters.

Steven Matz is the senior analyst at the ICC Counterfeiting Intelligence Bureau (CIB). He holds a Master of Laws in intellectual property from the University of London. He has worked for the CIB for five years and is responsible for producing its monthly confidential news bulletin, co-authoring special reports, running an international counterfeiting exhibition, developing new services and carrying out investigations. Prior to joining the CIB, Steven worked on numerous projects in the legal and business field. He is also a journalist and spent several years as a sub-editor for a national news-wire service.

The ICC Counterfeiting Intelligence Bureau (CIB), a specialist division of the International Chamber of Commerce, was formed in 1985 as a focal point for industries and other affected interests worldwide to fight the growing problem of counterfeiting. A non-profit-making membership organization, it comprises members from various countries and sectors, including large multi-national companies, trade associations, law firms and technology producers. The CIB is recognized by the British Home Office as a bona fide agency and has a formal Memorandum of Understanding with the World Customs Organization. Additionally, CIB investigators enjoy close professional links with senior officials in government and law enforcement agencies in many countries. Since its inception, the CIB has undertaken over 600 investigations in more than 35 countries into counterfeit products ranging from wall coverings and furniture to alcoholic beverages and pharmaceuticals.

Contact details: ICC Counterfeiting Intelligence Bureau, Maritime House, 1 Linton Road, Barking, Essex IG11 8HG, UK; tel: + 44 (0)20 8591 3000; fax: + 44 (0)20 8594 2833; e-mail: cib@icc-ccs.org.uk; Web site: www.icc-ccs.org.uk

Action against piracy

Brian Conlon at the Federation Against Copyright Theft (FACT) reports on the links between copyright theft and organized crime.

It is known that organized crime has now taken up film piracy as an effective means of generating funds for other serious criminal activity and for laundering money. The potential financial gain attained through counterfeiting is disproportionately favourable to the criminal compared with the risk of detection and effective prosecution.

The Asia–Pacific region and Pakistan are global centres of illicit production and exportation of counterfeit DVD film media. The method of importation into the UK is via airfreight parcels with optical discs easily secreted and packed in bulk. The production facilities are invariably small industrial units and home set-ups. Banks of CD 'burners' and videocassette recorders are able to produce thousands of units, with the price for blank media falling significantly in recent years. This provides a real attraction to would-be video pirates.

Not only is film piracy damaging the industry, it also hits the consumer, as more often than not the pirate version of any film is substandard and often defective, and a poor relation to the genuine article. For example, fake DVDs are often produced using a camcorder version filmed in an auditorium or other analogue source material, although some high-quality copies do originate from the studios themselves. Second-generation or copied VHS tapes are produced on recycled or 'degaussed' tapes, and are of inferior quality. A film pirate manufactures or imports the rogue films at a fraction of the cost of the genuine article.

It is not just the Hollywood film studios and their UK counterparts in distribution that are affected by film piracy. Local supporting businesses such as video dealers and rental outlets, printers, packers and delivery services, to name but a few, all suffer. Piracy harms UK jobs, evades the Inland Revenue thus harming UK investment, and limits the development of the UK film industry.

Illegal copies, which are usually sold by fly-by-night dealers at car boot fairs and street markets, are increasingly well packaged but with poor quality sound, colour and visual clarity. Lottery-funded UK film successes *Bend It Like Beckham*, *Gosford Park* and *28 Days Later* have all been targeted by DVD pirates, and pirate copies of Hollywood blockbusters *The Hulk, Terminator 3, Pirates of the Caribbean* and the UK-filmed *Tomb Raider 2* were available before their actual UK cinema release.

Individual street dealers are often the public front of organized criminals who use the proceeds to fund their other activities. According to the Intellectual Property Crime section of the FBI Web site, 'There is also strong evidence that organized criminal groups have moved into IP (Intellectual Property) crime and that they are using the profits generated from these crimes to facilitate other legal activities.'

A massive increase of over 400 per cent in the seizure of counterfeit films in 2003 demonstrates that piracy is not easily defeated. An issue of great concern to the Federation Against Copyright Theft (FACT) is the direct link between the money raised from intellectual property fraud and the funding of organized crime and terrorism rings. All the major anti-piracy trade bodies are reporting a huge rise in the level of fake products being smuggled into the UK. FACT seized almost 1.8 million pirated DVDs last year, a rise of 405 per cent on the previous year, and an amount that could have deprived the film industry of £440 million in lost revenue. The significant increase in seized goods in 2003 indicates that piracy is a booming trade. However, these figures only represent a small proportion of the counterfeit products entering the country. With technology advancing at a rapid rate and the uptake of broadband both in the office and in homes, our Internet investigation team has witnessed an increase in counterfeit traffic.

Last year we identified piracy moving from VHS to DVD. We predict that 2004 will definitely see a rise in Internet fraud piracy, although the successful import business of counterfeit DVDs from Asia and the Far East will still provide us with the biggest problem. The BBC recently recognized that illegal copies of its products were beginning to surface more frequently than in the past. In particular, substandard versions of popular DVD titles such as *Only Fools and Horses* and *The Office* are being sold on the Internet and at markets and car boot sales. In a bid to protect its business, and safeguard the best interests of its talent and consumers alike, the BBC turned to FACT.

FACT is pleased to welcome the support of the BBC as a new member. It means we can now prosecute on its behalf when our investigators seize products. FACT is also working closely with other industry members. A series of countywide raids conducted earlier this year by police and Trading Standards with assistance from FACT and BPI disabled a massive organized crime piracy syndicate. By going after the root of the problem we have been able to dramatically reduce the availability of pirated material across the UK.

Another huge achievement for FACT last year was the complete shutdown of Hackney market following a major public order operation involving senior FACT investigators and 85 Metropolitan police from Stoke Newington police division. The market had become notorious in recent years as one of the worst centres for the sale of counterfeit and stolen goods, particularly counterfeit DVDs. Our investigation team filmed undercover footage, later aired on prime-time television, showing the unhindered sale of fake/stolen goods, imitation firearms, crossbows, mobile phone unlocking/cloning and also blatant display of hardcore, unclassified pornography. FACT investigators spent months evidencing the inside workings of the market and the relationship between operators and illicit traders that would deal with the centre of distribution once and for all. The closure of Hackney market represents the FACT strategy for 2004. We will be hitting market owners and controllers hard, with the message: 'Get your house in order, or face prosecution and complete shut-down.'

FACT is not the only organization taking the issue of piracy seriously. The excellent work undertaken by the Alliance Against Counterfeit and Piracy has made government ministers finally provide us with a serious response. FACT has worked with partner organizations to form an Intellectual Property Crime Group backed by the Patent Office. This is a step in the right direction. However, it reinforces our view that the industry must unite and work closely together if we are going to stamp out piracy and organized crime for good.

The Federation Against Copyright Theft (FACT) is an investigative and representative organization funded by its members to combat all forms of film/video/DVD piracy, particularly copyright infringement, trade mark abuse, counterfeiting and product mishandling. FACT assists all statutory law enforcement authorities such as the police, trading standards officers and HM Customs and Excise officers to investigate and act against film piracy. The company operates under the world-wide umbrella organization the Motion Picture Association (MPA). Essentially FACT is an enforcement body protecting the film and satellite industries within the UK.

Intellectual property insurance

In a knowledge-based economy, insurers are designing cover for intellectual property, reports Peter Roedling at Hiscox.

For many years elements of intellectual property (IP) insurance have been incorporated in other insurance policy forms. Notably professional indemnity policies have provided defence cover for allegations of unintentional infringement arising from the practising of the particular profession. However, with the trend toward a knowledge-based economy, insurers have responded by identifying and responding to the need for specific intellectual property insurance, and designing specific covers aimed at these risks and for a wider client base than just traditional professions.

In broad terms cover is now available to anyone, as most commercial activities have the possibility of infringing the IP rights of others. Retailers, manufacturers, importers, designers, sports and leisure concerns might all unwittingly fall foul of the IP rights of others.

With IP assets showing up as intangibles on the balance sheet, they now have a more prominent part in the value of an enterprise. Because of this the owner is likely to be more concerned than in the past with protecting IP assets, as will be shareholders. This in turn leads to actions against those alleged to have infringed property rights.

Covers available

Essentially the two main liability related covers are for, one, defence and two, pursuit or enforcement.

Some innovative first-party covers are emerging to protect an insured from loss of revenue directly related to the loss of its specified IP, from its being compelled to pay unexpected royalties, and in the worse case from its being the subject of an injunction stopping its infringing activity. These 'own loss' policies are too 'state of the art' and new for it to be possible to make any valuable comment on them at this time.

Defence

This should become a ubiquitous coverage as it is not necessary for an insured to have any of its own IP in order to infringe that of others. In time this policy will become as commonplace as public, product or employers' liability cover. Looking at the award levels in the United States for infringement, it is surprising this is not already the case.

Pursuit

This cover provides access to the funding of legal and expert costs to enforce the insured's rights against others who are infringing them. The specific IP is scheduled, and generally consists of rights capable of registration such as patents, trade marks and designs, although specific copyrights and unregistered trade marks could be identified for cover.

An alternative to this cover is for an organization to buy an 'after the event' insurance policy when it becomes aware of an infringement. These are considerably more expensive, and cover availability will depend very much on the facts related to the infringement. They do not provide a predictable degree of cover for a pre-agreed price as is the case with the pursuit covers.

Buyer's checklist

As these policies are new and postdate the times when 'industry standard' wordings proliferated, there can be considerable difference between the insurance products on offer. This also helps account for the divergence in pricing among insurers in this area. The list below identifies some of the main features to consider when buying these policies.

Defence coverage

■ Does the policy provide damages as well as defence costs (legal and expert fees)? Some policies purely provide defence costs.

- Is the policy limit adequate bearing in mind the insured's activities and their volume? Consult with an insurance broker for benchmarking against peer organizations.
- Are the territorial and applicable courts provisions in line with the exposures? As many IP rights are granted by territory and have to be defended or enforced country by country in individual legal systems, does the policy match the exposures? As an example, if the organization supplies goods to Australia, would the policy defend it in an Australian court if it was claimed that those goods infringed an Australian patent?
- Exactly what activities are protected by the policy? While it is becoming common for Internet and e-mail IP exposures to be covered under the emerging cyber liability policies, IP policies should cover all the goods or products the organization offers for sale in the market. This will usually include the instructions for use and the packaging (but not separate advertising, which could be insured under a commercial general liability policy). Not all policies cover all of the insured's products however, and this point needs careful attention.
- Does the insurer offer any IP risk management advice? This shows its commitment to this highly technical area, and is a useful sign that it will know the best ways to handle any claims made against the insured. Quite often simple amendments to sale, supply or employment contracts can greatly reduce an insured's IP exposure.

Pursuit coverage

- All insurers have some mechanism in their wordings that requires there to be reasonable prospects of success in any legal action commenced. This insurance is not intended for a last throw of the dice, little or no chance situation. However, insurers should ensure that it is clear on reading the policy how this will operate. In case a dispute arises between insured and insurer over this issue, there should be a cost-effective resolution procedure outlined.
- While the expectation is that the enforcement case will be won, should the action fail, does the policy cover any award of costs against the plaintiff? This cover is important, as without it a large cost could be left uninsured.
- The limit sought should be sufficient to cover the organization's own legal and expert costs as well as those of its opponents. See above.
- As only granted IP can be enforced, what mechanism does the policy provide for handling infringements where the formal IP rights have not yet been granted? It should be possible to lodge the discovered potential infringement with the insurer.
- Is the premium for the period full and final? Some policies provide investigation costs only and charge an additional un-predetermined premium to take the action to court.

General points

■ Often, contractual agreements will determine who takes responsibility for defence or pursuit related to the IP elements of the contract. Does the policy have a mechanism to address this?

■ IP litigation is a complex area. Does the insurer have specialized claims handlers in this area? The experienced claims handler will have contacts with the legal experts relevant to the type of action in the appropriate country, and will understand the issues at the heart of the dispute.

The insurance premiums charged reflect the degree of cover given, the going cost of awards, legal and expert costs and the frequency of claims. Improvements in the courts to streamline the process, and increased roles for the Patent Office in re-examination and infringement determination, should all act to bring the cost element down. Risk management should play its role in reducing the frequency of defence actions, and the very existence of the pursuit policies should deter the unconcerned infringer, again reducing the frequency of claims. The outcome? Better prospects for inventors and creators to enjoy the benefits awarded them by the IP legislation, and less damage to balance sheets arising from unintentionally infringing the rights of others. There should also be reducing insurance costs as the improvements start to show in insurers' claims experience.

Peter Roedling is Manager of Intellectual Property Insurance at Hiscox. For further information tel: 020 7448 6211; Web site: www.hiscox.com

Dispute resolution

Litigation is generally a last resort in IP disputes, says Bruce Alexander at Boult Wade Tennant. Most cases are settled through negotiation, mediation or arbitration.

This section is concerned with the resolution of disputes arising from or relating to IP.

The means of resolving such disputes fall into three broad areas:

- criminal law;
- civil law;
- resolution without litigation.

Various legislation in English law provides that certain infringements of IP rights are criminal offences, and the criminal law therefore provides sanctions against such infringements. Criminal actions against IP infringers are necessarily taken by suitable authorized bodies, primarily trading standards officers and the Customs and Excise service in the UK. The criminal provisions apply primarily in the areas of piracy and counterfeiting.

The civil law also provides a framework of laws defining what constitutes infringements of various IP rights. Each of the Patents Act 1977, the Trade Marks Act 1994 and the Copyright, Designs and Patents Act 1988 (dealing with registered designs and unregistered design right) sets out a definition of what constitutes infringement of the rights registered under those Acts. The civil law provides a framework for enforcement of those rights through litigation in the courts, primarily the

High Court in London and the Patents County Court. This section deals with the third area listed above, that is, the resolution of disputes without resorting to litigation.

The sort of disputes involved

The very title 'dispute resolution' presupposes that a dispute exists. That is, there is a falling out between two parties. The main form of dispute with which this section is concerned therefore arises from the situation where an IP owner is aware of an activity or anticipates an activity, usually by a competitor or would-be competitor, that the rights owner believes is, or would be, an infringement of one or more of its IP rights.

The infringement might be of one of the following registered rights:

■ patent;
■ registered trade mark;
■ registered design;
■ plant variety.

The infringement might also be of an unregistered right falling within one of the following headings:

■ infringement of unregistered design right;
■ misuse of confidential information;
■ infringement of copyright;
■ passing off (abuse of a common-law or unregistered trade mark).

Finally the dispute might arise from IP without involving a direct infringement of IP rights, and fall into the following categories:

■ trade libel;
■ breach of contract/licence agreement;
■ breach of undertaking.

These last two categories apply only where there is an existing contract or agreement between two parties and one party believes that the other party is in breach of one or more of the terms of that agreement.

Ways to resolve the dispute

Once it is established that there is a dispute between two parties, there are a number of ways in which the dispute may be resolved:

- negotiation;
- mediation;
- arbitration;
- litigation.

Mediation and arbitration are usually collectively referred to as 'alternative dispute resolution'.

The basic premise of both negotiation and alternative dispute resolution is that most disputes are capable of resolution in a way that will provide a satisfactory commercial compromise for the parties without recourse to the courts. Litigation should generally be regarded as a last resort.

This basic premise is borne out by the reality. Many disputes involving IP can arise. It is impossible to quantify this, but disputes other than those of a trivial nature must run into many thousands per annum. Of those disputes, no more than a few hundred result in any form of litigation, or even the start of litigation by the issue of proceedings. Of those cases where proceedings are started, the vast majority are settled before going to trial. Only a very small number of cases, measured in no more than tens, reach trial in the High Court or the Patents County Court.

It is perhaps a popular misconception that, if a dispute arises, one party immediately sues another. In reality, there are strong incentives to try to settle disputes without resorting to litigation.

First, there is the cost and uncertainty of litigation. IP disputes taken through to trial in the High Court or Patents County Court typically involve costs to both parties of many tens of thousands of pounds. While the winning party might recover a significant proportion of its costs, recovery is never 100 per cent. Litigation also involves a substantial amount of executive time and other hidden costs to the litigants.

The outcome of litigation is nearly always uncertain. It is axiomatic that, in a dispute involving rational parties, if the outcome of litigation to resolve that dispute is certain and this is apparent to both parties, a settlement will quickly follow. Cases that reach trial are therefore inevitably cases in which the outcome is uncertain. The uncertainty in litigation does not only arise from the final outcome. Litigation takes time, sometimes running into years rather than months, and both parties are left with uncertainty until the litigation is concluded.

A second, and perhaps more important, incentive to try to settle without litigation is the attitude of the courts following the Wolff Report and the reforms of civil procedure after that report. Put simply, it is now a requirement for would-be litigants that they first try to settle the dispute in question by means other than litigation, and that they have exhausted any reasonable settlement possibility before commencing litigation. If litigation is started and the courts are not satisfied that reasonable attempts have first been made to resolve the dispute, cost penalties may be imposed on one or other of the parties. Thus, there are strong incentives to attempt to resolve disputes through negotiation, mediation, or arbitration.

In essence, all three processes have the same essential features. They involve the parties and their aim is to identify commercial terms that will resolve a dispute, which are acceptable to both parties in the light of the relative strength or weakness of their positions.

Negotiation

Negotiation implies discussion between the parties, and this presupposes that the parties are prepared to talk to each other in order to resolve the dispute, either directly at face-to-face meetings involving executives of the parties or through intermediaries, for example, solicitors, patent or trade mark attorneys or other third parties.

Negotiations will be a normal first step in trying to resolve a dispute. Once the cause of the dispute has been identified and both parties have been advised by their own advisors of the relative strengths and weaknesses of their positions in the dispute, a usual first step will be to try to reach a negotiated settlement.

Negotiations might start following a specific offer from one side or the other to settle the dispute. For example, in a patent dispute, the patentee might be prepared to grant a licence to an infringer to allow the infringer to continue with its activities, and the negotiation will then revolve around the terms of the licence.

If negotiations are to be successful, it is important that each party prepares for negotiation and has fully analysed its position prior to the negotiations.

Each party must:

■ understand the merits of its legal position in relation to the dispute;
■ understand its own commercial strengths/weaknesses in the dispute and those of the other party;
■ have defined its objectives in the negotiations and its preferred outcomes;
■ have identified the points that it is not prepared to concede (deal breakers);
■ understand what it is able or willing to concede in the negotiations.

Clearly, if each party has gone through this process, it is unlikely that the initial objectives of both parties will match. Each party will be hoping to extract a little more from the negotiations than its own minimum requirements. Each party's objections must be based on a sensible analysis of the strengths and weaknesses of its position, but each party will hope to achieve a little more than its position necessarily merits.

A negotiated settlement of a dispute might be achieved in a single negotiation session, but far more usually will involve a number of offers and counter-offers, often spread over a significant time and a number of meetings or exchanges. Negotiation is not, of course, mutually exclusive from litigation or any other form of dispute resolution. Sometimes negotiations are only commenced after litigation has started or been threatened, and they can continue up until final resolution of the litigation. As discussed above, the vast majority of IP actions started in the courts are settled before coming to trial.

If negotiations are successful, they will result in a list of agreed points, and these will then usually be embodied in a settlement agreement, a binding contract between the parties.

Mediation

In a similar way to negotiation, mediation is a process conducted between the parties and involving a third party. However, in mediation, the third party is not a retained advisor to either of the parties in the dispute, but is an independent person. The aim of the mediator, a neutral intermediary, is to help the parties to reach a settlement of their dispute acceptable to both parties and, therefore, mutually satisfactory.

Mediators are trained individuals holding a qualification that certifies that they bring certain skills in resolving disputes and in bringing parties together to the mediation process. Various organizations offer accredited mediators, for example, the World Intellectual Property Organization (WIPO) Arbitration and Mediation Centre.

The mediator's task is to try to identify and clarify the issues between the parties and help the parties to resolve those issues. There are a number of characteristics of mediation:

- *Mediation is a non-binding procedure.* A mediator cannot impose a settlement on the parties, and equally, a party to a mediation cannot be forced to accept an outcome suggested by the mediator. The mediator is not a judge and not a decision maker. The mediator's role is to assist the parties in reaching a settlement of a dispute that is acceptable to both of them.
- *Mediation is controlled by the parties.* As the mediator has no power to impose a settlement on the parties, it follows that the parties control the process. Even if the parties have agreed to mediation, if either party feels that the mediation is unlikely to result in an acceptable settlement of the dispute, the parties are free to abandon the process at any time.
- *Mediation is a confidential procedure.* The mediator has no power to force parties to disclose information that they wish to keep confidential.

If the parties agree to disclose confidential information in order to assist in trying to reach a resolution of the dispute, then that disclosure will normally be under condition that it is kept confidential by all parties and will not be used in any other context, for example, in subsequent litigation if mediation is unsuccessful.

If a mediator is successful in getting the parties to reach agreement on a settlement of the dispute, then in the same way as at the conclusion of negotiations, that settlement is normally recorded in a binding contract signed by the parties.

Arbitration

Arbitration is a procedure in which, by agreement of the parties, a dispute is submitted to one or more arbitrators who make a decision on the dispute. Arbitration can be binding on the parties, so that the arbitrator's decision is final, or it can be non-binding. A non-binding arbitration is far less usual. Generally, parties will opt for arbitration in order to reach a binding resolution of their dispute without resorting to litigation and the courts.

The principal characteristics of arbitration are:

- *Arbitration is consensual.* An arbitration can only take place if the parties have agreed to the process. Sometimes this is agreed on an ad hoc basis when a particular dispute arises, and sometimes, particularly in contractual disputes, arbitration is the dispute resolution procedure provided for in the contract. Once the parties have agreed to an arbitration procedure, it will take its course. Unlike mediation, one or other party cannot withdraw during the process.
- *Arbitration is neutral.* An aim of arbitration is to ensure that both parties view it as a fair and neutral process without favour to either party. For this reason, parties to an arbitration will normally agree on a neutral venue, and such things as applicable law and languages will be chosen to ensure no advantage to either party.
- Equally, *the arbitrator is usually chosen by agreement between the parties* and may be one or more persons, usually with knowledge in the law concerned. In arbitrations arising from contractual disputes, the arbitration clause in the contract might provide for the appointment of an arbitrator from a specific source, for example, by the President of the Law Society, in the absence of agreement between the parties as to an arbitrator.
- *Arbitration is confidential.* In the same way as mediation, usual arbitration rules will specifically protect the confidentiality of information provided to the arbitrator by both parties. That information will be used

solely in the arbitration, to allow the arbitrator to reach a decision, and will not be available to the parties for any other use.

The arbitration decision is binding and easy to enforce. In most arbitrations, the arbitrator's decision will be both binding on the parties and final, that is not subject to an appeal to any court or any other tribunal. Many arbitrations are international in nature, involving parties in different jurisdictions. Arbitration awards are usually enforced under an international convention, to which many countries are signatories, which allows national courts to enforce the awards and allows them to be disputed or set aside only in very limited circumstances.

Arbitration is therefore by its nature more similar to litigation than to mediation or negotiation, but it can be less costly and time-consuming than litigation while retaining the advantage that it does provide a final decision on the dispute.

Bruce Alexander is a partner at Boult Wade Tennant, European Patent and Trade Mark Attorneys and Chartered Patent Attorneys, and is President of the Chartered Institute of Patent Attorneys (CIPA). He provides strategic advice to clients on trade mark policy and management of trade mark portfolios world-wide, including major retail plans. He has particular experience in merchandising sporting events and personalities, and other institutions undertaking major trade mark filing programmes. He also assists clients on enforcement through the courts and otherwise. He has substantial experience of practice before the European Community Trade Mark Office, especially in resolving trade mark oppositions. For further details contact: balexander@boult.com

Index